D1521235

STRAND PRICE
$5.00

GENERAL
MATTHEW B. RIDGWAY

Bibliographies of Battles and Leaders

The Battle of Antietam and the Maryland Campaign of 1862: A Bibliography
D. Scott Hartwig

The Central Pacific Campaign, 1943-1944: A Bibliography
James T. Controvich

American Warplanes 1908-1988: A Bibliography
Myron J. Smith, Jr.

Pearl Harbor: A Bibliography
Myron J. Smith, Jr.

The Battles of Coral Sea and Midway, 1942: A Selected Bibliography
Myron J. Smith, Jr.

The Battle of Jutland: A Bibliography
Eugene L. Rasor

The Falklands/Malvinas Campaign: A Bibliography
Eugene L. Rasor

The Normandy Campaign, 1944: A Selected Bibliography
Colin F. Baxter

The Spanish Armada of 1588: Historiography and Annotated Bibliography
Eugene L. Rasor

GENERAL
MATTHEW B. RIDGWAY

An Annotated Bibliography

Compiled by
Paul M. Edwards

Bibliographies of Battles and Leaders, Number 8
Myron J. Smith, Jr., Series Adviser

Greenwood Press
Westport, Connecticut • London

Library of Congress Cataloging-in-Publication Data

Edwards, Paul M.
    General Matthew B. Ridgway : an annotated bibliography / compiled
by Paul M. Edwards.
       p.   cm.—(Bibliographies of battles and leaders, ISSN
1056-7410 ; no. 8)
    Includes bibliographical references (p.) and indexes.
    ISBN 0-313-28739-2 (alk. paper)
    1. Ridgway, Matthew B. (Matthew Bunker), 1895-   —Bibliography.
I. Title. II. Series.
Z8745.25.E39   1993
[E745.R52]
355'.0092—dc20   93-10832
[B]

British Library Cataloguing in Publication Data is available.

Library of Congress Catalog Card Number: 93-10832
ISBN: 0-313-28739-2
ISSN: 1056-7410

First published in 1993

Greenwood Press, 88 Post Road West, Westport, CT 06881
An imprint of Greenwood Publishing Group, Inc.

Printed in the United States of America

The paper used in this book complies with the
Permanent Paper Standard issued by the National
Information Standards Organization (Z39.48-1984).

10 9 8 7 6 5 4 3 2 1

CONTENTS

vi   Contents

SERIES FOREWORD

The Greeks at Thermopylae, the Crusades, the Armada campaign, Trafalgar, Verdun, Gettysburg, El Alamein, Pork Chop Hill, Khe Sahn, the Falklands, and "Desert Storm" are only a few of the many campaigns and battles, large and small, which have been fought down through the ages. Of course, each of these operations had leaders ranging in quality from Leonidas at Thermopylae to the group think of Vietnam and all featured diverse strategy, tactics, and weaponry. It appears to be mankind's unhappy lot that war has been and apparently will for sometime continue to be a growth industry, despite centuries of horror-filled record-keeping and preventative lessons available for the learning. With only a few exceptions, monographic bibliographies of individual battles and leaders (our series title admittedly, is borrowed from the famous American Civil War history), campaigns and weapons have not been compiled previously. Contributors to this series while thus breaking new ground have also constructed works suitable for wide general audiences. These tools may profitably by employed at every level from high school through graduate university and by the casual researcher/buff as well as the dedicated scholar.

Each volume begins with a narrative overview of the topic designed to place its subject within the context of specific wars, societies, and times; this introduction evaluates the significance of the leader, battle, or technology under study. Each work points to key archival and document collections as well as printed primary and secondary sources. Citations are numbered, allowing easy access via the index(es). Individual volumes may present discussion of their citations in styles ranging from bibliographical essays to individually annotated entries and some titles provide chronologies and suitable appendix(es).

It is my hope as editor that these bibliographies of battles and leaders will enable broad audiences to select and work with the best items available within literature and to benefit from the wisdom of some of today's leading military scholars.

Myron J. Smith, Jr., Series Adviser
Tusculum College
Greeneville, Tennessee

PREFACE

General Matthew B. Ridgway served the United States for decades, playing key roles and providing leadership in both military and diplomatic missions. His ideas helped to form the concept of airborne warfare. His organizational and planning skills greatly influenced the preparation for, and execution of, World War II. His dramatic leadership of United Nations troops in Korea finally held the Chinese Communist Forces. As NATO Commander, and Army Chief of Staff, he was instrumental in America's expanding role in world affairs.

The two basic periods of his active service, World War II and the Korean War, represent the extremes of bibliographic availability. During World War II Ridgway was a senior officer, but not of such rank to encourage major historical coverage. However, the wide interest in World War II, and in airborne activities in particular, provides extensive resources from which to draw doxographical information concerning General Ridgway and his military involvement.

As we near the fiftieth anniversary of the end of World War II, declassified and other new materials, continue to become available.

General Ridgway played a public and vital role during the Korean War, as commander of the Eighth Army and as General Douglas MacArthur's replacement in the Far East Command. And much of this is reflected in the literature.

The study of the Korean War, however, is still limited. The shortage is not so much in terms of official records, nor the availability of official action reports. Rather there is a shortage of interpretation, analysis, personal narrations, memoirs, general and special histories, and reevaluations.

Secondary materials dealing with the Korean War, and thus with General Ridgway's role in it, are just now appearing, and much of the necessary analysis and evaluation is still being formed.

Materials Included

Included in this bibliography are materials written by Matthew B. Ridgway, written about him in one of his many roles, or written about events in which his role is significantly discussed. Included also are the official and unofficial records of the commands he held, and the unit activities over which he presided.

Since there is no complete biography of General Ridgway, some collections of biographical materials have been included. By necessity these research lists include only those works originally in English or available in translation.

During both World War II and the Korean War ground units were required by regulation to keep official records. At most levels, from artillery battalions to divisions, corps or armies, official (staff) historians were at work.

Their records consist of action reports, war diaries, battle narratives, daily reports and intelligence information. Air records were often kept in association with the above. Air Force, Navy and Marine units also kept like materials.

These records are at the Army's Center of Military History, in conjunction with the National Archives. The heart of the material was used in the publication of the official series, <u>The United States Army in World War II</u>

and <u>The United States Army in Korea</u>, but a good deal remains in typescript form.   Most of the messages between the Joint Chiefs of Staff and General Headquarters are available in the Modern Military Records Branch of the National Archives.

Unit reports from the European Command are generally available at the U. S. Army Military History Institute but the best collection of published history is the New York Public Library.

For the Korean War the reports of the Eighth Army in Korea, as well as its components (I, IX, X Corps and the six combat divisions) are located at the National depository in Suitland, Maryland.

Oral histories of leading military commanders, as well as interviews with Ridgway and those who knew him, are to be found at the U.S. Marine Corps History (Division) Museum at the Washington Navy yard, in the Special Collections of Mitchell Memorial Library, at the MacArthur Memorial Archives and the Harry S. Truman Presidential Library at Independence, Missouri.   The Center for the Study of the Korean Conflict, also located in Independence, concentrates on the private papers, orders, oral tapes, photographs, maps, etc. of the individual soldiers.

Both World War II and Korea were much photographed and Ridgway had a propensity for the camera.   However a very small percentage of these photographs appear in print.   Most photographs can be located at the Still Picture Division, Main Archives, and at the Defense Audiovisual Agencies, Still Photographic Depository, Anacostia Naval Station, Washington, D. C.   Maps are preserved at the Cartographic and Architectural Branch, Special Archives, National Archives, Alexandria, Virginia.

Materials Excluded

It is estimated that over fourteen thousand tons of documents are available for the researcher into World War II.   When a significant biography of Ridgway is written, these records will need to be searched for the occasional reference.   However, no effort has been made to identify this still generally unindexed material.

Other than for occasional reference I have excluded collections of biographies, picture books, "table top" works, general histories in which Ridgway is mentioned only in passing (and there are hundreds), news items in newspapers (available New York Public Library on microfilm), accounts primarily directed at his wife or members of his family, legal documents, personal letters of non-military nature, or items which unduly repeat materials found elsewhere.

Period Covered

General Ridgway was born in 1895 and that date identifies the extreme of this bibliography. He retired in 1955 marking the end of any official position, though materials written about him after that time have been included. Obviously there is little in the public record about the early days of his life. As a general rule the amount of coverage increases in direct proportion to his age and stature until, in post-retirement, he gradually slipped from the public mind. No effort has been made to trace his roots or to follow his family.

Organization

This study has been organized along two basic formats. The first is archival materials which include primary archival and published documents.

The other includes secondary sources which are divided into general reference materials (dictionaries and research aids); materials written by and about Ridgway; the World War II era (with subdivisions for individual command responsibilities); the period between the wars; the Korean War period (with Eighth and Far Eastern Commands); NATO; Army Chief of Staff, and retirement years.

Special sources are listed together and include dissertations and films.

The work concludes with a list of the periodicals reviewed, an author and subject index.

ACKNOWLEDGMENTS

The development of a research aid of this type requires the help of many persons; librarians, archivists, research associates as well as correspondents. Among the many who provided valuable assistance as a matter of their daily routine, I must acknowledge with appreciation the librarians and staff of the Kansas City, Missouri, Public Library, Mid-Continent Public Library of Jackson County, Missouri, the library of the University of Missouri at Kansas City, Washburn University in Topeka, Kansas, the Denver Public Library, Linda Hall Library of Kansas City, Baker University Library at Baldwin, Kansas, Chicago Public Library, New York Public Library, Sterling C. Evans Library at Texas A & M University, and the collections at the Center for the Study of the Korean War, Independence, Missouri.

Extraordinary thanks go to Louise A. Arnold-Friend, reference historian at the U. S. Army Military History Institute, Carlisle Barracks; to the librarian and staff at the Command and General Staff Library at Fort Leavenworth; Mary Lou Goodyear at Sterling C. Evans Library, Dr. Benedict Zobrist and his staff at the Harry S. Truman Presidential Library; and Dr. Tom Peterman of Park College Library, Kansas City, Missouri.

Without question the aid and assistance of Joni
Wilson, executive secretary, The Center for the Study of
the Korean Conflict, must be recognized. Her generous
offering of painstaking research, careful checking, and
patient skills were essential to the completion of this
work.

Thanks are given also to Professor Myron J. Smith,
Jr. of Tusculum College Library, Greeneville, Tennessee,
who worked with me in clearly identifying the topic and
to Mildred Vasan at Greenwood Press. The assistance of
Roger Revell, Joan Blair, and the Baker University
graduate class on the history of the Korean War is
acknowledged.

Numerous named and unknown authors and contributors
have made this bibliography possible, their writings and
reports on the events and life of Matthew B. Ridgway
have been rewarding to review.

And lastly to Matthew B. Ridgway, thank you.

Paul M. Edwards, Ph.D.
Independence, Missouri

CHRONOLOGY

1895:   3 March   Born Fort Monroe, Virginia of Thomas R.
                  and Ruth Starbuck Bunker

1913:   14 June   Enters West Point

1917:   20 April Graduated West Point, 2nd Lieutenant

                  Married Julia Blount

        May   Promoted 1st Lieutenant
                  Assigned 3rd Infantry on Mexican
                  border

        August   Temporary Captain

1918:   Began service as instructor of Romance
                  Language at West Point

1919:   July   Became permanent Captain

                  Assigned to train Olympic squad

                  Joined General Frank McCoy, 3rd Brigade
                  in Nicaragua on diplomatic mission

1925:   Co. Commander, 15th Infantry

1926:   Co. Commander, 9th Infantry

1927-1928:   Secretary, American Electoral
                 Commission, Nicaragua

1929: March   Member, Bolivian-Paraguayan
                 Conciliation Commission

1929-1930:   Infantry School (advanced course) at
                 Fort Benning, Georgia

1930: June   Married Margaret (Peggy) Howard Wilson
                 Dabney

1932: October   Promoted Major

1932-1933:   Technical Advisor to Governor General,
                 Philippines

1933-1935:   Two year course at Command and Staff
                 College, Fort Leavenworth, Kansas

1935: June   Assistant Chief of Staff, 6th Corps

1936: March   Deputy Chief of Staff, 2nd Army

                 Planned the Louisiana Maneuvers for
                 summer

1936-1937:   Army War College, Washington

1937-1939:   Assistant Chief of Staff, Fourth Army,
                 Presidio

1939-1942:   War Plans Division, War Department,
                 General Staff

1939:   Trip to Brazil with General Marshall

1940: July   Promoted Lieutenant Colonel

1941: December   Temporary Colonel

	December	Hq. Army Chief of Staff under General George C. Marshall, Washington, DC
1942:	January	Temporary Brigadier General
1942:	25 March	82nd Airborne Division activated, Deputy Division Commander
	26 June	Command 82nd Airborne Division
	August	Temporary Major General
1943:	10 May	82nd Division at Casablanca
1943:	9-10 July	Gela, Italy, executed Husky Number Two
1943:	1 August	Sorrento Ridge
1943:	11 Sept	Distinguished Service Medal
1943:	13 Sept	Assault at Salerno, Italy
1943:	Sept	Forms Composite Unit, 82nd and British 23 Armored, 600 Rangers under Ridgway take Naples
1943:	November	82nd, minus 504th, returned to Scotland to train
1943:	2 Dec	Award of the Legion of Merit
1944:	6 June	Ridgway makes only combat jump
1944:	19 July	Award of Oak-leaf cluster to DSC
	July	82nd returns to England
	2 Aug	First Allied Airborne Army formed
	27 Aug	Takes command of XVIII Corps (82nd, 101st, 17th)
	16 Sept	Dropped close to Arnhem

Sept	At Bastogne, Ridgway and staff, with three guards, cross Rhine
Dec	Battle of the Bulge
1945: May	XVIII Airborne Corps altered for transfer to Pacific War. Canceled
	Commander Luzon Area Command
1945: June	Temporary Lieutenant General, Commander Mediterranean Theater, Deputy SACMed
1946-1948:	Senior US Army member Military Staff Committee United Nations
	Chairman, Inter-American Defense Board
1947: June	Married Mary Anthony (Penny) one son, Matthew, Jr.
1947-1949:	Commander in Chief, Caribbean Defense Command
1949: October	Deputy Chief of Staff for Operations and Administration
1950: 25 June	Invasion of South Korea
5 July	Task Force Smith makes first American contact
1 August	UN Forces in Pusan Perimeter
15 Sept	Inchon Landing
30 Sept	ROK, 3rd Division crosses 38th Parallel
26 Nov	200,000 Chinese attack the Eighth Army north of the Chongchon
11 Dec	1st Marine and 7th Army Division withdrawn at Hungham

22 Dec	Ridgway notified he would replace Walker, killed in jeep accident
26 Dec	Ridgway takes command Eighth Army
1951: 3-4 Jan	Retreat causes evacuation of Seoul
25 Jan	Eighth Army and ROK take offensive
14 March	Eighth Army reoccupies Seoul
11 April	Ridgway succeeds MacArthur as CINCUNC
May	Promoted to General
23 May	Jacob Malik, Deputy Foreign Commisar of Soviet Union proposes cease fire
30 June	Ridgway, on order from Washington, broadcasts to Chinese UN readiness to discuss truce
2 Nov	Ridgway orders Van Fleet to cease offensive and begin defensive operations
1952: 12 May	Ridgway takes over NATO command from Eisenhower
1953: 19 July	Negotiators at Panmunjom reach agreement
27 July	Armistice signed
1953-1955:	Chief of Staff, U. S. Army
1955: 30 June	Retired from active duty
1957-1960:	Chairman, board of Trustees, Mellon Institute of Industrial Research
1956:	Published Soldier
1967:	Published The Korean War

1968:   As one of Johnson's "Wise Men" he
                     advocated deescalation of the Vietnam
                     War

1993: 26 July   Matthew B. Ridgway dies on the eve of
                     the fortieth anniversary of the signing
                     of the armistice at Panmunjom.

BIOGRAPHY

Matthew Bunker Ridgway was born in Fort Monroe, Virginia, on the 3rd of March 1895. His father, Colonel Thomas Ridgway, was a regular army artillery commander who had served in the Boxer Rebellion. Growing up at army bases all over the United States, Matthew Ridgway graduated from English High School in Boston, Massachusetts, in 1912. He attended West Point and graduated from the Academy, standing 56th in a class of 139, in April of 1917, receiving his commission as a second lieutenant in the infantry. Following graduation he married Julia Carolline Blount on April 20, 1917. They eventually had two daughters, Constance and Shirley.

The young officer's first assignment was as a company officer at Camp Eagle Pass along the Texas-Mexican border during a time of consistent conflict. He was promoted to first lieutenant in May of 1917 and to temporary captain on 5th of August of the same year. Anxious over his failure to get overseas, Ridgway served with the 3rd Infantry in Texas until September of 1918.

In that year Ridgway returned to West Point as an instructor in the Romance languages and the executive for the athletic department, then as graduate manager of athletics. At this time he considered his assignment at the Academy as the "death knell of his military career." But he completed his time at West Point with ability and efficiency, making friends and acquaintances which would last a lifetime. He was promoted to the permanent rank of captain on July 18, 1919.

After completing the prescribed course at the Infantry School, Fort Benning, Georgia, Ridgway served successful tours as a troop commander in such varied assignments as Texas, China, Nicaragua, and the Canal Zone. Like so many young officers in the peace-time army, he served fifteen different assignments in seventeen years.

His first overseas assignment was as a company commander with the 15th Infantry in Tientsin, China. On his return he was appointed company commander, then regimental adjutant with the 9th Infantry at Fort Sam Houston, Texas. From December 1927 till February of 1929 he served under General Frank McCoy with the American Electoral Commission in Nicaragua, returning to graduate in June of 1930 from the Advanced Course Infantry School. He served with the Thirty-third Infantry at the Panama Canal Zone.

He was divorced in 1930, later marrying Margaret (Peggy) Howard Wilson Dabney in June of that year. He adopted Margaret's daughter, Virginia Ann, in 1936. Occasional assignments led to service with the Bolivia-Paraguay Conciliation Commission where his language and diplomatic skills were developed. He was promoted to temporary major on October 1, 1932.

In the spring of 1932 Major Ridgway was ordered to the Philippine Island to act as liaison to the Insular Government and as technical advisor to Governor Theodore Roosevelt, Jr. The following August he received an appointment to the Command and General Staff School at Fort Leavenworth, Kansas. Following his graduation he served for a period as Assistant Chief of Staff with 6th Corps in Chicago then in the same assignment for

Operations, with Second Army. In March he became Deputy Chief of Staff of Second Army.

He graduated from the Army War College and after a period on the staff of the Fourth Army in San Francisco, he joined the War Plans Division of the War Department in September of 1939. He was promoted to the rank of lieutenant colonel July 1, 1940, to temporary colonel on December 11, 1941, and to temporary brigadier general on January 15, 1942.

When the 82nd infantry division was reactivated at Camp Clairborne, Louisiana in March of 1942 General Matthew Ridgway received a long awaited troop command as deputy Division Commander under General Omar N. Bradley. Bradley was a good friend and mentor and when he was ordered to another divisional command, Ridgway succeeded him as a two-star general (August 6, 1942) in command of the 82nd. He oversaw the division's conversion to an airborne unit.

Just a year after activation, the 82nd Airborne Division arrived in Casablanca to begin training in North Africa. There Ridgway took part in planning and directing the airborne invasion of Sicily. The 82nd Airborne Division entered combat during the invasion with General George S. Patton's Seventh Army. Elements of the 82nd, primarily James Gavin's 505th Regimental Combat Team, parachuted behind enemy lines at Gela on the 9th and 10th of July, 1943, in the first major Allied airborne assault, and the largest night drop, in history.

The questionable success of the airborne attack in Sicily led many to doubt the effectiveness of the specialized unit. Ridgway was instrumental in developing new understandings of the use and deployment of airborne, and aided in reorganizational and training efforts which supported the airborne participation in the invasion of France. Ridgway jumped with his troops into Normandy on D-Day, 6 June, 1944 in his first combat jump.

Following the creation of the Allied First Airborne Army, Ridgway was appointed to command the Eighteenth Airborne Corps in August of 1944. In this role he commanded military operations in and around Eindhoven, Holland, during the Ardennes campaign in Belgium, at the Ruhr "pocket" crossing, the breaching of the Elbe, in stemming the German offensive during the battle of the Bulge in December of 1944, and at the advance junction with Soviet troops on the Baltic on May 2, 1945.

Recently promoted to lieutenant general (temporary) Ridgway returned to the United States with the Eighteenth Corps in preparation for the use of airborne troops in the invasion of Japan. He headed to the Philippines to arrange airborne participation in the invasion, but the war ended while he was in route.

In October of 1945 Ridgway was given command of the Mediterranean theater of operations. Then he was appointed as General of the Army Dwight D. Eisenhower's representative to the Military Staff Committee of the United Nations. As the army's representative he was a principle figure in drafting what was later to be the statement of relations for armed forces at the disposal of the Security Council. He served from January 1946 to June of 1948.

His assignments took him to London in January of 1946 as an advisor for the United States civil delegation to the UN Assembly. Ridgway was divorced in 1947 and married Mary Princess (Penny) Anthony on December 13, 1947. He met Penny while she was senior secretary and he was director of the Inter-American Defense Board. Their son, Matthew Jr. was born in 1949.

In a series of post-war assignments General Ridgway served with the Inter-American Defense Board, and as military aid to President Miguel Aleman of Mexico during the 1947 Pan American Conference. Ridgway, along with experts from Chile and Argentina, defined the Western Hemisphere security zone.

In July 1948 Ridgway was named to command the Caribbean Defense Command; a year later, in October, he assumed the responsibilities of deputy chief of staff of the army under General J. Lawton Collins.

When war came to Korea, in June of 1950, Ridgway became General Collin's principle advisor and effectively was the operations officer for the army's role in Korea.

It was just before Christmas, 1950, when he received word he was to succeed General Walton H. Walker as commander of the Eighth Army in Korea. Walker had been killed in a jeep accident. Given less than 24 hours to leave Washington and assume his new command, he met General MacArthur at the Dai Ichi on Christmas. He was given command, no longer divided, of 365,000 men, and told to defeat the Chinese.

Once in place he moved quickly to revitalize the UN troops which were seriously demoralized by the rapid success of the Chinese Communist forces. Things were so bad the Joint Chiefs of Staff had drawn up secret plans for "operation bugout", an evacuation of the peninsula. Ridgway began immediately to regain the confidence of troops, and their officers, personally visiting command headquarters to meet with those serving on the line.

Assessing the battle conditions, he allowed his troops to pull back to ground where his technologically superior forces could hold. He operated on the belief that the most effective response was to destroy the enemy's army and he pushed that effort rather than simply seeking to regain land. Then in the early days of 1951 his revitalized troops took the initiative and, with an army of nearly 400,000 men, moved toward Seoul.

A large man, balding and weathered, sophisticated and professional, meticulous over details he was nevertheless a soldier's soldier. Known by his troops as "Old Iron Tits" because of the grenades strapped to his harness, he managed to rise above the dramatics, giving instead a sense of honest involvement.

Shortly after World War II a _Time_ magazine description of the General suggested he looks like a Roman senator and lives like a Spartan hoplite. He was, at this time, of rugged build, six feet and about 190 pounds, with brown hair and brown eyes.(1) He kept in shape with a routine of running and chopping wood.

Considered by Russell Spurr as "America's most underrated military genius"(2) Ridgway's counterattacks marked the decisive point in the struggle for Korea. Ceasefire calls began and shortly thereafter the conflict settled into a military stalemate with minor movement either North or South.

In April of 1951 Ridgway succeeded MacArthur, ousted by President Truman after several years of disagreement, as head of the Far East Command, receiving promotion to general in May. In this assignment General Ridgway assumed four major roles: deputy for the 17 UN Nations fighting in Korea; commander of US Forces in the Far East; military governor of Japan, and director of United Nations negotiations for a truce in Korea.

Under his leadership the Korean armistice talks assumed a more serious tone, beginning July of 1951. They continued under Vice Admiral C. Turner Joy, Ridgway's recommendation as the primary representative. Under Ridgway's direction a treaty was created and finally signed at Panmunjom in 1953.

In May 1952 Ridgway succeeded General Dwight D. Eisenhower as supreme commander of NATO Forces in Europe. In June of that year he received the additional command of all U.S. Forces in Europe. A different leader than Eisenhower, he nevertheless proved to be a capable commander and diplomat in this exacting post.

1. _Time_ 47 (April 2, 1945) 27.

2. Russell Spurr. _Enter the Dragon: China's Undeclared War against the US in Korea, 1950-1951_. New York: Newmarket Press, 1988.

On October 1, 1953 he was named Chief of Staff of the U S Army by President Eisenhower, and served until his retirement. A long term advocate for the ground army, and a prophet warning of the difficulties of too much reliance on technological warfare, Ridgway voiced a deep concern about American involvement in Vietnam. On June 30, 1955 General Matthew B. Ridgway retired from active service, bringing to a close forty-two years of military and diplomatic service performed in over thirty countries.

General Ridgway received thirty-three military and governmental decorations in all; among these he holds the Distinguished Service Cross (with oak-leaf cluster); the Distinguished Service Medal (with three oak-leaf-clusters); Silver Star (with oak-leaf-cluster); Legion of Merit; Bronze Star Medal "V" (with oak-leaf-cluster); Purple Heart; and 11 foreign awards.

Following his retirement Matthew Ridgway served as executive officer or director of several firms. From 1957 to 1960 he was Chairman of the Board of Trustees of the Mellon Institute of Industrial Research.

He continued to be an active opponent of America's involvement in Vietnam. He had warned President Eisenhower that an Asian war could not be won by air power alone. Long after he left active duty he openly advocated a "phased-withdrawal" of American troops. During Lyndon Johnson's term, he served as one of the President's "wise men", representing his views at the famed "crisis of conscience" conference in March, 1968.

The "wise men" known officially as the Senior Informal Advisory Group on Vietnam consisted of Dean Acheson, George Ball, McGeorge Bundy, Douglas Dillon, Cyrus Vance, Arthur Dean, John McCloy, Robert Murphy, Arthur Goldberg, Henry Cabot Lodge, Abe Fortas, General Omar Bradley, General Maxwell Taylor, and General Matthew Ridgway.

Matthew Bunker Ridgway died quietly in his sleep at his home in Pennsylvania on the 26th of July, 1993.

GENERAL
MATTHEW B. RIDGWAY

ARCHIVES AND DOCUMENTS

ARCHIVES AND DEPOSITORIES

NATO

NATO Archives

SHAPE Press Releases, Paris, France, 1 June 1952
to December 1953.

Private Collections

The Center for the Study of the Korean Conflict, Independence, Missouri

Personal papers of individual soldiers,
photographs, orders, personal narratives.

Citadel, Charleston, South Carolina

General Mark W. Clark Papers.

University of Texas, El Paso, Texas

Samuel L. A. Marshall vast research library and
personal papers.

United Nations

United Nations Archives, Still Picture Division, Main Archives, Washington, DC

Still photographs of the Korean War.

United States

Cartographic and Archives Branch, Special Archives Division, National Archives, Alexandria, Virginia

Maps and overlays from World War II and the Korean
War Period

Combined Arms Research Library, United States Command and General Staff College, Fort Leavenworth, Kansas.

USAF Airborne Operations, World War II and
  Korean War   (March 1962) (Official use only)
Ridgway, Matthew B.   "Combat Leadership of
  Larger Units." 2 reels: Lecture (May 19,
  1966) (currently classified for official use only).

Defense Audiovisual Agencies, Still Photographic Depository, Building No. 168, Anacostia Naval Station, Washington, DC

Still photographs of World War II and the Korean
War period

Document Section: Library of Congress, Washington, DC

Robert P. Patterson Papers (1930-1952), Under
Secretary (1940-1945) and Secretary of War (1945-
1947), these papers contain reports from
Commanding Officers including General Ridgway

Dwight D. Eisenhower Presidential Library, Abilene, Kansas

Dwight D. Eisenhower (Pre-presidential) Papers
1916 - 1952
Norman D. Cota Papers (28th Infantry
Division, Europe)
Frank A. Keating Papers (102nd Infantry
Division, Europe)

Franklin D. Roosevelt, Presidential Library, Hyde Park, New York

Correspondence files (by name of subject) wartime
commands

George C. Marshall Research Library, Virginia Military Institute, Lexington, Virginia

General Matthew B. Ridgway Collection
General George C. Marshall Collection, Chief-of-
Staff World War II

Harry S. Truman Presidential Library, Independence, Missouri

Harry S. Truman Papers (President)
Dean Acheson Papers
Matthew J. Connell Papers
Korean War File
John L. McKee (European Command)

U. S. Korean War, Selected Document from
  Department of State and Department of Defense
U. S. Army Unit Diaries, 1944-1951
Oral Histories:
  General Lucius D. Clay.
  John H. Muccio, Ambassador to Korea, 1949 -
    1952

Hoover Institute on War, Stanford University, Stanford, California

Miscellaneous File, Korea, Accession No. TS
  Korea U58
Admiral Charles Turner Joy Papers and Diaries,
  Chairman of the UN negotiation team
North Korean Propaganda materials

Legislative and Diplomatic Branch, National Archives, Washington, DC

3600 pages of the records of the hearings
  concerning the release of General Douglas
  MacArthur
Reports, statements and other documents
  concerning the political decisions relating to
  the Korean War

MacArthur Memorial Archives, Norfolk, Virginia

Most of the important messages between MacArthur
  and the Joint Chiefs of Staff have been
  published, but other papers, including telexes
  between MacArthur and Ridgway have not been
  published. Especially useful records of General
  Headquarters, UN Command 1945-51. RG 6. RG 7.
  RG 8 Hq. USAF in Korea

Modern Military Records Branch, National Archives, Suitland Road, Suitland, Maryland

Millions of pages of official reports from
  Eighth Army and its components. Included are
  the tactical narrative section of the monthly
  command reports of 8th Army, I, IX, X corps as
  well as the six combat divisions and 19
  regiments
War Diaries (through November of 1950) and
  Command Reports (after November 1950) with
  supporting documents. These are monthly
  summaries of actions prepared at all levels of
  command.
Military History Section of Headquarters, Far
  East Command. "History of the Korean War,
  Chronology, 25 June 1950 - 31 December 1951"
25th Division Records, RFG 407, Box 3746 et al
3rd Division Records, RFG 407, Box 2889 et al
Okinawa Battalions, RFG 407, Boxes 147, 743.
Office of the Chief of Naval Operations, July
  1941-January 1942, RG 38, 301-763-7410
Office of the Quartermaster General, RG 92, 301-
  763-7410
United States Theaters of War, RG 332, 301-763-
  7410
U.S. Army Command, selected, RG 338, 301-763-
  7410
Headquarters, U. S. Air Force (Air Staff) RG
  341, 202-501-5385

Modern Military Records Branch, National Archives, Washington, DC

Roy Appleman's collection of letters and
  comments from participants in the Korean War. A
  very valuable and generally unused collection of
  memoirs and mainly first-hand accounts.
Messages between the Joint Chiefs of Staff and
  General Headquarters in Tokyo. Record Group 218.
  Most of these are published in Foreign Relations
  of the United States Vol VII, 1951, part 1 & 2

"Record of Actions Taken by the Joint Chiefs of
    Staff Relative to the United Nations Operations
    in Korea from 25 June 1950 to 11 April 1951,
    Prepared by Them" (April 30, 1951) 107 pages
XXIV Corps Historical File, Records Group 332,
    44 boxes
Intelligence (G-2) Library, United States Army,
    Record Group 319
Intelligence Summaries, North Korean, Record
    Group 739, "P" File 1946, 51
Records of the Joint Chiefs of Staff, battle
    studies prepared by the eight Historical
    Detachments of Eighth Army
Records of the Joint Chiefs of Staff 1942-1953,
    Records Group 218; geographic files arranged
    alphabetically

National Archives, Branch Offices, Microfilm Offerings, Washington, DC

Records of War Production Board, RG 179
World War II Crimes Records, RG 238
World War II, Collection of Seized Enemy
    Records, RG 242

National Personnel Records Center, Military Personnel Records, St. Louis, Missouri

Military personnel (201) files

Naval Historical Center, Office of Navy History, Washington, DC

Oral Histories:
  Robert L. Dennison
  Daniel V. Gallery
  Malcolm Schoeffel
  George Miller
  John S. Thach
  Fitzhugh Lee

Walter W. O. Ansel
David McDonald
D. D. Griffin
Commander-in-Chief, U. S. Pacific Fleet <u>Interim</u>
  <u>Evaluation Reports</u> (6)
<u>Daily Operation Orders</u>, <u>Command Reports</u>, and <u>War</u>
  <u>Diaries</u>
General Headquarters, Tokyo. <u>History of the</u>
  <u>North Korean Army</u>

U. S. Army Center of Military History, Washington, DC

Numerous battle narratives compiled by official
  army historians. Some published in Gugeler's
  <u>Combat Actions in Korea</u> but longer and more
  detailed accounts can be found here.
Diaries:
  John P. Lucas
  Floyd Parks (First Allied Airborne
    Headquarters)
  William C. Sylvan (First Army Headquarters)
Manuscripts:
  Ralph P. Eaton (82nd Airborne in
    Mediterranean)
  Charles LaChaussee (unpublished history of the 1st
    Battalion, 517th Parachute Infantry Regiment)

U. S. Army Military History Institute, Carlisle Barracks, Pennsylvania

General Matthew B. Ridgway, archives. Sixty-six
  boxes, 82nd Airborne Division Archives, XVIII
  Airborne Diaries, After-action reports, maps,
  and unit histories, substantial biographical
  materials, speeches, newspaper and magazine
  clippings
Ridgway Papers, Box 17, S-3, Public Information
  Officer news account Eighth Army, 13 December
  1950
Mark W. Clark Papers
James K. Woolnough Papers

Edward M. Almond Papers
Maxwell D. Taylor Papers
Frank E. Lowe Papers 1947 - 1985
Tapes of interviews conducted by Clay Blair for
  A General's Life and Ridgway's Paratroopers
  including interviews with Matthew B. Ridgway, J.
  Lawton Collins, Mark W. Clark, Maxwell D. Taylor,
  and James M. Gavin.
Clay Blair collection, documents.
  "High Level Correspondence." Eighth Army,
  Forgotten War Files, Blair Collection, Box 41.

  Joint Chiefs of Staff, History, Korean War,
  Forgotten War Files, Blair Collection, Box 47.

  "Alphabetical Files: R-S." Omar N. Bradley Files,
  Blair Collection, Box 21.

  Chronological Notes, Units, Alphabetical Files,
  Ridgway's Paratroopers File, Blair Collection,
  Boxes 27-35.

  Miscellaneous Files, Maps, Ridgway's Paratroopers
  File, Blair Collection, Box C-7.

  Name File, Ridgway's Paratroopers File, Blair
  Collection, Box C-8.

Clay Blair collection, oral histories
  taken by Clay and Joan Blair, in conjunction
  with the preparation for Ridgway's Paratroopers,
  donated to USAMHI. These tapes contain
  considerable information about Ridgway and his
  World War II activities, beyond that available in
  Clay Blair's book on the subject.

Beauchamp, Charles E.	1 side
Casey, James A.	2 sides
Clark, Mark W.	2 sides
Cochran, Alexander S. (paper)	1 side
Collins, J. Lawton	2 sides
Eaton, Ralph P. (Doc)	5 sides
Ellis, John T. (Glider Study)	2 sides

Gavin, James M.	8 sides
Kroos, Arthur G.	6 sides
Lewin, Richard (rebuttal of Cochran)	1 side
Matthews, Willis	4 sides
Moorman, Frank W.	6 sides
Norris, Frank W.	2 sides
Ray, William J.	3 sides
Ridgway, Matthew B.	12 sides
Sanford, Teddy H.	3 sides
Sherman, Eleanor	1 side
Surles, Alexander D.	4 sides
Swenson, John H.	2 sides
Taylor, Maxwell D.	5 sides
Thomas, David E.	1 side
Trussell, John B.	4 sides
Turner, Paul L.	1 side
Winton, Walter F.	6 sides
Yarborough, William P.	2 sides
Oral History Notes (Almond, Hode, Hull, Pace, Taylor)	2 sides
82nd Airborne Division History	6 sides
Special Diary	3 sides
Airborne Museum	1 side

Materials from Ridgway's inner circle, Frank W. Moorman, A. Day Surles, Walter F. Winton and Emory S. Adams.

Samuel L. A. Marshall Korean Papers.

Matthew B. Ridgway (Elton/Caulfield Interviews)

Omar N. Bradley - Military Reference Branch, National Archives and Records Center is the depository for the Department of Defense. They have Bradley's classified materials in RG 330. Unclassified are at West Point.

John A. Hixson (Lt. Col.) and Dr. Benjamin Franklin Cooling Combined Operations in Peace and War. unpublished, 1982.

U. S. Marine Corps History (Division) and Museum, Navy Yard, Washington, DC

The Aide-Memoire and Flight Log of Major General Oliver P. Smith, 1950-1951

Oral History Reports:
  Oliver P. Smith, Commander, First Marine
    Division
  Alpha A. Bowser, G-3, Commander, First Marine
    Division, 1950-1951
  Edward A. Craig, Acting Division Commander,
    First Marine Division
  Gerald C. Thomas, Commander, First Marine
    Division
Diary File (Battalions) First Marine Division

Washington National Records Center, Washington, DC

Far East Command (FEC) "Chinese Communist
  Military Operations in Korea." Intelligence
  Digest 35 (November 1-15, 1952) 44-51. National
  Archives, Federal Records Center, Record Group
  407, Box 766

Yale University Library, New Haven, New York

Roger W. Tulby Journals, State Department
  Press Officer, 1950 Assistant Press Secretary
  White House, 1952 White House Press Secretary
Henry L. Stimson, Secretary of War, 1940-1945

PUBLISHED DOCUMENTS

BOOKS

001   American Foreign Policy: Basic Documents, 1950-1955, Part XV, Korea. Washington, DC: Department of State Publications, 1957.
     Basic documents of the outbreak, the policies, and the continuing execution of the Korean war, many of which are related to Ridgway's years as Eighth Army Commander and Commander Far East.   Primarily document pages 2527-2738.

002 American Foreign Policy: Basic Document, 1950-1955, Part I-IX.   Washington, DC: Department of State Publications, 1957.
     Primary documents dealing with NATO during those years when Ridgway was serving as NATO Commander. Well indexed, but especially document pages 1504-1707.

003   Blumenson, Martin.   The Patton Papers, 1940-1945. Volume II.   Boston: Houghton Mifflin Co., 1972-74. 889 pages, index, photographs.
     Discussion of the airborne invasion of Gela, Italy, and the danger of friendly fire on the planes carrying the airborne under Ridgway.   Includes Ridgway's explanation as to why no disciplinary action would be taken for the logistical failure of the air drop. 281-283.

004   Chandler, Alfred D. and Louis Galambos (editors). The Papers of Dwight David Eisenhower: The War Years. Five volumes. Baltimore: Johns Hopkins University Press, 1970.
     A carefully edited collection of the papers of General Eisenhower which provides primary documents dealing, in several incidents, with General Ridgway. In particular see documents 951, 2427, 2442, 2467, 2616-2617.

005 Cordier, Andrew W. and Wilder Foote. Public Papers of the Secretaries-General of the United Nations, Vol. 1, Trygve Lie, 1946-1953. New York: Columbia University Press, 1969. 535 pages, index.

Papers dealing with Ridgway's role in Korea, the United Nations support of Ridgway as MacArthur's replacement as the Far East Commander, Ridgway's public proposal to the North Koreans for ceasefire are all documented.   Includes UN support for Ridgway as a negotiator, and the report of the Secretary-General on the military efforts of the United Nations in Korea. 381, 391, 393, 453, 499.

006 Department of Defense, Semi-annual Reports of the Secretary of Defense, and Semi-annual Reports of the Secretary of the Army, Secretary of the Navy, Secretary of the Air Force, January 1 to June 30 and July 1 to December 30, 1950 through 1953. Washington, DC: Government Printing Office. 1950-1955.

These reports on military action are filed by field and theater commanders and include action reports by General Ridgway from his assignments with both Eighth Army in Korea and Far East Command.

007 Foreign Relations of the United States, 1950, Vol. VII, Korea.   Washington, DC: Department of State Publications, Office of the Historian, 1976.

Ridgway briefs Pentagon, December 3, 1950, (1323-24, 1330), Joint Chiefs Policy (99935), January 2, 1951, policy statement for withdrawal if necessary, Ridgway and MacArthur, (1625).

008 Foreign Relations of the United States, 1951, Vol II, Korea and China. Washington, DC: Department of State Publication, Office of the Historian, 1982.

This is a major source of primary materials dealing with the command of General Ridgway. The index of Ridgway entries occupies two pages.

009 Foreign Relations of the United States, 1952-53, Parts I and II, Korea and China. Washington, DC: Department of State Publications, Office of the Historian, 1984.
Major source of Ridgway materials dealing with both military and diplomatic efforts, which are carefully indexed.

010 Historical Report, U. S. Military Advisory Group to the Republic of Korea. (KMAG) Tokyo: Daito Art Printing Company, Limited, Public Information Office. 1 July 1949 to 31 December 1949.
Report of the Korean Military Advisory Group during the effort to build up an ROK army. The lack of clarity in a policy toward Korea is reflected in this effort.

011 Langsam, Walter C. (editor). Historic Documents of World War II. Princeton, New Jersey: Princeton University Press, 1958. 192 pages.
Primary documents of the military and political events of World War II. While brief and very selective this will expose some Ridgway understanding.

012 O'Neill, James E. and Robert W. Krauskopf (editors). World War II: An Account of Its Documents. Washington, DC: Harvard University Press, 1976. 269 pages.
Papers and proceedings of the Conference on Research on the Second World War, June 14-15, 1971, concerning the location, use, and extent of documents relating to World War II which are housed in the National Archives.

013 Public Papers of the Presidents of the United States, Harry S. Truman, 1950. Washington, DC: Government Printing Office, 1951.
Documents and letters during the Truman presidency which are basic to understanding the Ridgway period of the Korean War. Brief mention of Ridgway.

014   United Nations Documents, 1946-1960. Readex Microprint Edition. Readex, New York: Microprint Corporation, 1978.

Thousands of microfiche records and primary documents are available, each housed under separate headings for the General Assembly, Atomic Energy Commission, United Nations Administrative Tribunal, Disarmament Commission, Economic and Social Council, Security Council, United Nations Special Fund Governing Council, and Trustee Council. Ridgway's connection with the United Nations is apparent in these documents which, if they are to be used, require extensive work in the combined indexes, which are separately housed and on microfiche.

015   U. S. Congress, Senate, Foreign Relations and Armed Services Committees. Military Situation in the Far East. 5 volumes. 82nd Congress, 1st session, 1951.

This microfilm version of the report on the Far East, which is held at the Legislative and Diplomatic Branch, National Archives, is far more complete than the version published (1951) and listed under a separate heading.

016   U. S. Congress, Senate Hearing. Committee on Armed Services 82nd Congress, 2nd Session, 1952.

Highlights of the Armed Service Committee hearing for the promotion of Matthew B. Ridgway.

ARTICLES

017   "Discussion with General M. B. Ridgway re Far Eastern Situation, Koje-do Uprising of POW's and NATO Policies" 82nd Congress, 2nd Session (Microfilmed on Reel 45, Carnegie Library).

Ridgway reports to congress on the causes of, effects of, and potential solutions to the question of prisoner of war outbreaks; on the role of the United Nations and the NATO commander.

018   "General of the Army Douglas MacArthur and the American Policy in the Far East."   Joint statement by the Armed Forces Committee and the Committee on Foreign Relations, U. S. Senate, Senate Document No. 50, June 28, 1951

This significant statement about the dismissal of General MacArthur goes beyond that question and takes a really good look at the policies of the Korean conflict. Necessarily includes material on Ridgway and of interest to those studying him as MacArthur's replacement.

019   "Memorandum for the Record, Aug 15, 1950" Interlocking Subversion in Government Departments: Hearing Before the Subcommittee to Investigate the Administration of the Internal Security Act and Other International Security Laws.   83rd Congress, 2nd Session. Washington, DC: US Senate, 1954-1955. 2026-2027.

Ridgway memorandum concerning governmental confrontation and the increasingly hostile "search for communists" in the military. It was Ridgway's stand which blocked efforts to taint the military with the "communist" stain.

020 United Nations Command. "The Communist War in POW Camps: the Background of Incidents Among Communists Prisoners in Korea" (n.p) Headquarters United Nations and Far East Command, Military Intelligence Section, General Staff, 1953 (1) 34 (2) 6 (1) leaves, diagrams and notes.

Tries to identify and explain the extent of the communist influence in the numerous POW uprising, includes some brief analysis of the Koje-do and Ridgway's response.

021   "The United States and the Korean Problem" Documents 1943-1953, Government Printing Office, 1953.

A brief collection of materials that attempts to explain the reason for the war, America's involvement, and the political implications before, during, and after the war. Some Ridgway but most of this material has been covered elsewhere.

SECONDARY SOURCES

BIBLIOGRAPHIES, DICTIONARIES AND REFERENCES

BOOKS

022   The Army Almanac.   Harrisburg: The Stackpole
Company, 1959. 797 pages, name and topic indexes.
   Basic facts about the organization and management
of the U.S. Army.   General Ridgway is a significant
character in this collection with more than a dozen
entries in the wide index.

023 Beers, Henry P. Bibliographies in American History,
1942-1978.   2 volumes.   Woodbridge, Connecticut:
Research Publications, 1982.
   An extensive list of available bibliographies in
English on thousands of topics. Included are those about
units, battles, and events associated with Ridgway, as
well as Korean and NATO topics.   Primarily chapter 7.

024 Blanchard, Carroll H. Jr.   Korean War Bibliography
and Maps of Korea.   Albany, New York: Korean Conflict
Research Foundation, 1964. Subject and author index.
   The first publication of a very ambitious program
to collect and identify all materials dealing with the
Korean War.   His   subject   arrangement   is   somewhat
difficult, but he has identified some excellent
materials that do not appear elsewhere.   Dated.

025   Controvich, James T.   <u>United States Army Unit Histories: A Reference and Bibliography</u>. Manhattan, Kansas: Military Affairs/Aerospace Historian, 1983.

Includes some valuable information on units in World War II and Korea, as well as citations of ground participation, commanding generals, and an excellent bibliography.

026   Imperial War Museum Library. <u>The War in Korea, 1950-1953, A List of Selected References</u>. London: War Museum Library, 1961.

This mimeographed list includes more than 350 books, articles, and monographs in English on the Korean War. It includes references to both British and American units.

027 MacFarland, Keith D. <u>The Korean War: An Annotated Bibliography</u>. New York: Garland Publishers, 1986. 461 pages, subject and author index.

An excellent collection of materials dealing with the war, well arranged and easy to identify, cross referenced in index. The annotations are brief but crisp. In his citation he does not identify indexes in individual works. Other than the fact so much new materials have appeared in the past four years, this is a fine and useful research tool.

028   Matray, James I. <u>Historical Dictionary of the Korean War</u>. Westport, Connecticut: Greenwood Press, 1991. 648 pages, index, photographs, maps.

An excellent quick reference to the Korean War. Contains a good biography of Ridgway during the war plus numerous significant indexed entries. 405.

029   Palin, Charles C., and Dale Reed. <u>Guide to the Hoover Institution Archives</u>. Stanford, California: Hoover Institute Press, Stanford University, 1978.

The Hoover Library and Archives is so vast, and the combined references so interwoven, that anyone seeking to locate Ridgway materials would need this source to isolate subjects and events.

030   Park, Hong-Kyu.   The Korean War: An Annotated Bibliography. Marshall, Texas: Demmer Co., Inc., 1971. 29 pages, limited and dated.
A brief and very selective work which concentrates on Korean entries (in English).

031 A Revolutionary War: Korea and the Transformation of the Postwar World. Colorado Springs, Colorado: USAF Academy Library, Special Bibliography Series, No. 84, October 1992.
A brief but informative bibliography directed toward support of the idea the Korean War was more revolutionary than international.

032 Saunders, Jack. "Records in the National Archives Relating to Korea 1945-1950" Cumings, Bruce (editor). Child of Conflict. Seattle, Washington: University of Washington Press, 1983.   355 pages, index.
This essay provides an excellent guide to materials that have become available concerning the Korean War. The declassification has come about through the use of the Freedom of Information Act.

033 Summers, Harry G. Jr. Korean War Almanac. New York: Facts on File, 1990. 330 pages, index, photographs, maps.
An alphabetical listing of major events and personalities in the Korean War.   Besides being an excellent handy reference for Ridgway's Korean period, it contains a good short biography. This includes Summers' analysis of why Ridgway was successful in transforming the Eighth US Army during the "turn around". 232-234.

034 Tunney, Christopher. A Biographical Dictionary of World War II. London: Dent, 1972.
This work designed for quick reference provides the standard bibliographical reference for Ridgway up to the end of World War II.   In the absence of an official biography this is one of the better sources on Ridgway's early years. 161-162.

035 William, Mary H. (compiler). U. S. Army in World War II: Chronology 1941-1945. Washington, DC: Office of the Chief of Military History, Department of the Army, Government Printing Office, 1960. 660 pages, index.

A carefully prepared day by day account of the military activities of World War II. While each entry is limited it does provide a good overview of what is happening, when, and by whom, including Ridgway's somewhat confusing role as XVIII Corps Commander.

BOOKS AND ARTICLES BY MATTHEW B. RIDGWAY

BOOKS

036 Ridgway, Matthew B. The Korean War. Garden City, New York: Doubleday and Company, 1967. 291 pages, index, photographs, maps and appendix.

Ridgway tells his own story of the struggle to re-establish the dispirited army he inherited, and turning the tide. Not as subjective as Soldier it provides much usable information. Appendix includes personal letters and orders dealing with the highlights of his command.

037 Ridgway, Matthew B. Matthew B. Ridgway, Jr., 27 April 1949 - 1 July 1971. Pittsburgh, Pennsylvania: Private Printing, 1972. 62 pages.

A father's tribute to his son through reproduced letters. Included here because of the degree to which young Matthew figured in the official coverage of the General. The young man was killed in a sporting accident.

038 Ridgway, Matthew B. Pictorial History of the Korean War. St. Louis: Veterans' Historical Book Service, 1954. 386 pages, photographs, maps.

The Combined Arms Research Library lists Ridgway as the author of this good collection of photographs and comment. There is no indication on the book of its author, however it contains Ridgway's and Clark's reports.

039 Ridgway, Matthew B. (as told to Harold H. Martin).
Soldier: The Memoirs of Matthew B. Ridgway. New York:
Harper & Bros., 1956. 351 pages.
   Recalls his World War II experience in some depth
including the much publicized 82nd Airborne. He also
deals with his controversies with Secretary of Defense
Wilson, and includes his Korean experience. Very
critical of both leaders and procedures on some
occasions.

ARTICLES

040 Ridgway, Matthew B. "Address" Department of State
Bulletin (November 1952) 817-819.
   Excerpts of an address made before the Pilgrims
Dinner at London in which Ridgway outlines the military
concept behind NATO: "an adequate though small covering
force of land, sea, and air, always on guard, capable of
meeting any sudden onslaught and of parrying any
potentially disastrous or decisive thrusts." He makes
his case in the light of history, and pushes for speed
in preparation.

041 Ridgway, Matthew B. "An Airborne Corps Operation"
Military Review 25 (November 1945) 14-16.
   Discusses the technical aspects of the British
crossing of the Rhine at Wesel, as it was supported by
the US XVIII Airborne Corps.

042 Ridgway, Matthew B. "The Army Chief of Staff" Army
Information Digest 8 (November 1953) 3-6.
   A clear statement by the chief of staff concerning
the coming reorganization of the defense department, and
how it would affect the army.

043 Ridgway, Matthew B. "The Army's Basic Role"
Infantry 49 (April 1959) 25-26.
   Pushing his primary theme, Ridgway talks about the
ultimate decisive role in warfare, and discusses the
fact that the objective of a sound army can not be
reached quickly. The basic reason for war is to control
land and people and ground troops are needed to do that.

044   Ridgway, Matthew B. "The Army's Role in National Defense" <u>Army Information Digest</u> 9 (May 1954) 21-30.
      The text of an address delivered to the Cleveland Post, Army Ordinance Association in 1954. Ridgway warns that despite all the great advances in weapons, armies still function, and win due to the combination of men, material and morale.

045   Ridgway, Matthew B. "Army Troops and Public Relations" <u>Army Information Digest</u> 9 (August 1954) 3-6.
      The army's leading spokesman acknowledges that troop information and community relations are vital to the success of the armed forces, urging more communication between the military and the community, as well as between headquarters and troops.

046   Ridgway, Matthew B. "Foreword" in C. Turner Joy with Allen E. Goodman (editor). <u>Negotiating While Fighting: The Diary of Admiral C. Turner Joy at the Korean Armistice Conference</u>. Stanford, California: Hoover Institute Press, 1978.
      A supportive forward to this armistice account by the negotiator Ridgway personally selected to lead the armistice talks.

047   Ridgway, Matthew B. "Founders Day, 1971" <u>Assembly</u> (Spring 1971) 21.
      Ridgway, speaking to a West Point crowd, suggests the academy has been the inexhaustible source of integrity within the military.

048   Ridgway, Matthew B. "General Ridgway Reports on Korea" (Interview) <u>US News</u> 32 (June 6, 1952) 26.
      In an interview with Senator Richard B. Russell, Chairman of the Armed Forces Committee, Ridgway comments on the prison revolt at Koje-do. Ridgway applauded the discipline of the guards, yet advocates stronger measures be used to control rioting prisoners. The key, he points out, lies in control of the hard line communists.

049   Ridgway, Matthew B.   "General Ridgway speaks..."
Infantry School Quarterly   44 (January 1954) 6-14.
    After becoming Army Chief of Staff Ridgway spoke to
the quarterly concerning Army organization, the budget,
and how the affairs of the office of Army Chief would be
conducted.   In light of his later actions this was a
very important statement about his views of military
organization and management.

050   Ridgway, Matthew B.   "How Europe's Defense Looks to
Me"   Saturday Evening Post 226 (October 10,   1953) 28-
29, 143-144.
    On leaving NATO command, General Matthew B. Ridgway
praises the growth of NATO efficiency.   But he makes it
very clear that any relaxing at this point could weaken
NATO "at the most dangerous hour Europe has faced since
WW II."   Ridgway argues against allowing NATO to drift.
Significant statement concerning future defense policy
in Europe.

051   Ridgway, Matthew B.   "The Indispensable Weapon"
Combat Forces Journal 4:6 (January 1954) 9.
    Notwithstanding   the   value   of   mechanical   and
technological weapons, the safety of America lies in the
minds, hearts, and hands of the American fighting men.

052   Ridgway, Matthew B.   "Indochina: Disengaging"
Foreign Affairs 49 (July 1971) 583-592.
    Warns   that   withdrawal   from   Vietnam   must   be
accomplished only after the return of all POWs is
guaranteed, and then all troops must be withdrawn.

053 Ridgway, Matthew B. "The Issue Now Joined" Life 30
(February 5, 1951) 27. Time 57 (February 5, 1951) 7.
    A printing of Ridgway's address to the troops on
why they were in Korea. This was reprinted in dozens of
popular commercial publications, the forms of which vary
slightly.

054   Ridgway, Matthew B.   "Korea and Japan, Military Operations, Armistice Negotiations, Relations with People" (Address: May 22, 1952) <u>Vital Speeches</u> 18 (June 15, 1952) 540-543.

An address before Congress, on returning from the Far East command, in which he praises the Armed Forces of the United States and of the United Nations; issues a warning about communist fabrications and says peace is now up to them; and warns of a "Red Threat" in Japan.

055   Ridgway, Matthew B. "The Korean War, Issues and Policies" Manuscript, Center of Military History, Washington, DC. 360+ pages.

A book length document developed by Ridgway concerning the political, as well as military, aspects of fighting the Korean War. Has been used extensively by Billy C. Mossman in <u>Ebb and Flow</u>, but is available for further research.

056   Ridgway, Matthew B. "Leadership" <u>Military Review</u> 46 (October 1966) 40-49.

An address concerning large unit command and leadership, delivered 19 May 1966 at Command and General Staff College.

057   Ridgway, Matthew B. "Letter" <u>The Christian Century</u> (November 21, 1951) 1346.

In a letter to the Laymen's Movement for a Christian World, Ridgway reminds them of the need for prayers for the nation, for the fight against communism, and for the representatives of the United Nations. An editorial note suggests it did not arrive in time for the celebration of Laymen's Sunday (October 21, 1951). A rare and interesting insight into Ridgway's religious beliefs.

058   Ridgway, Matthew B.   "Letter"   <u>Combat Forces Journal</u> 4:5 (December 1953) 17.

Letter, dated October 23, 1953, to General Decker, of the Association of the US Army, thanking him for the editorial work in integrating the various military journals in the <u>Combat Forces Journal</u>.

059 Ridgway, Matthew B.   "Loyalty, Cliques, Criticism"
Combat Forces Journal 4:4 (November 1953) 38.
     At his first staff conference as Army Chief of
Staff, Ridgway outlines a style demanding loyalty and
standing against cliques and unwarranted criticism.

060 Ridgway, Matthew B. "Military Factors and National
Policy" Army Information Digest 9 (October 1954) 3-4.
     A strong military force frees the hands of the
civilian leaders to guide the nation through the
pitfalls of international action. National policy is
not made by the military, but the military advisor can
support the civilian decision.

061 Ridgway, Matthew B. "Military Responsibilities"
Weigley, Russell Frank (editor). The American Military:
Readings in the History of the Military: American
Society. Reading, Massachusetts: Addison-Wesley, 1969.
xix, 184 pages.
     Primarily excerpts from his book The Korean War in
which Ridgway, with subtle suggestions about affairs in
the Far East command, defends the policy of the primacy
of civilian authority over the military.

062 Ridgway, Matthew B. (edited by Harold H. Martin).
"My Battle in War and Peace: The Korean War"   Saturday
Evening Post 228 (January 21) 17-19; (January 28) 34-
5+; (February 4) 26-7+; (February 11) 30+; (February 18)
30+; (February 25, 1956) 30+.
     The General's account of assuming command of the US
Eighth Army in December 1950.   He admitted to some
general confusion, but writes of how the military
situation was brought under control.

063 Ridgway, Matthew B.   "On Assuming Command of the
Eighth Army" Harding, Harold F. (editor).   The Age of
Danger: Major Speeches of American Problems. New York:
Random House, 1952.
     The full text of Ridgway's speech on assuming
command of EUSAK on 26 December 1950. This brief effort
addresses the question "Why are we here?" -- "What are
we fighting for?" The text of this speech, or parts of
it, appear in several periodicals as well. 138-140.

064 Ridgway, Matthew B. "Pull-out, All-out, or Stand Fast in Vietnam?" Look (April 5, 1966) 78-85.
    Our military obligation in Korea was a moral one, Ridgway acknowledged, but our obligation in Vietnam is a treaty obligation. And while it must be honored, there is no clear cut military or political goal in Vietnam. Two things we need to remember from our lesson in Korea; the idea of sanctuaries are hard to take but are useful in the political sense, and we cannot enter into agreements with the communists unless very clear. This article contains Ridgway's nine principles for involvement in Vietnam.

065   Ridgway, Matthew B.   "The Reason Why" Army Information Digest 6 (March 1951) 34-35.
    Text of a broadcast delivered on ABC radio 25 January 1951, in which Ridgway urges that it is time for defense, not only in Korea, but defense against the potential war spots around the world.

066   Ridgway, Matthew B. "Report of U. N. Command Operations in Korea" Department of State Bulletin (#30, 31, 32, February 18, 1952, 266) (#33, March 10, 1952, 395) (#34, March 17, 1952, 430) (#35, March 31, 1952, 521) (#36, 37, April 14, 1952, 594) (#38, May 5, 1952, 715).
    These reports follow the early stages of negotiation in which Ridgway plays a vital role. He reports on the communist response to early proposals, and opens up the growing problem of prisoner return.

067   Ridgway, Matthew B. "Report of U. N. Command Operations in Korea" Department of State Bulletin (May 19, 1952) 788-789.
    This is the basic text of report #39 [April 15, 1952] and is of significance because it identifies the number of persons, 40,000, required for rotation (in and out of Korea) if an armistice agreement was to be signed. This report gives an excellent view of Ridgway's determination in the question of the armistice, and seems somewhat strange in light of Ridgway's personal feelings in the matter.

068   Ridgway, Matthew B.   "Report on the Far East" (Address: May 22, 1952) Department of State Bulletin, [also reported in Vital Speeches] 26 (June 9, 1952) 924-927.
     Report before a joint session of Congress, May 22, 1952.   In it Ridgway reports on three topics: The conduct of military operations in Korea, the armistice negotiations, and American relations with the Japanese people.

069 Ridgway, Matthew B. "Ridgway Clarifies the Issues" America 87 (June 7, 1952) 262-3.
     Ridgway, speaking to the Senate Armed Forces Committee, clarified an issue that had been misprinted in a previous issue of America.   He asserts that contrary to the America editorial, "our relative combat potential is perhaps not as favorable now as it was last year." But, to bomb Manchuria at this point would bring the Soviet air force into the fight.

070 Ridgway, Matthew B.   "Second Anniversary of SHAPE as an Operational Headquarters" Department of State Bulletin 28 (June 29 1955) 899-904.
     A brief, but informative commentary on the organizational difficulties of SHAPE, but the vast achievement made during the two years of his involvement. Warns of letting down the guard.

071 Ridgway, Matthew B.   "Speech" May 30, 1952, Paris: Public Information Division, SHAPE, pages 1-21.
     The text of the speech Ridgway delivered at the command turnover ceremonies in May of 1952.

072 Ridgway, Matthew B.   "Speech" Paris: SHAPE Press Release, Mimeographed.
     Rough copy of speech delivered by Ridgway at Ste. Mere Eglise, France, on the 6th of June 1952 which tied the victory of the European War with the need for military organization and control in NATO.

073 Ridgway, Matthew B. "The Statesman and the Soldier:
Foreign Policy Has a Military Aspect as Well as a
Peaceful Aspect" Vital Speeches 20 (September 1, 1954)
674-676.

This address, delivered to the American Assembly in
Harriman, New York on 30 July 1954, is directed toward
the support of a strong ground army. While he agrees
that saber-rattling is unproductive, and that the
deliberate use of war as a diplomatic devise is both
"immoral and dangerous" he makes note of the fact that
wars, if necessary, are won by the domination over other
human beings and the territory they inhabit, and this is
only done by ground forces.

074 Ridgway, Matthew B. "Sustaining NATO's Objectives"
Department of State Bulletin (June 22, 1953) 869-872.

Ridgway affirms his determination to preserve the
peace and freedom of Europe, and thus of America,
through a commitment to unified command and efficiency.
Ridgway accepts the challenge and acknowledges need of
his command to always prepare for military intervention,
but work for peace.

075 Ridgway, Matthew B. "Tribute to Artillery" Combat
Forces Journal 2 (October 1951) 12.

Short statement penned by the new chief of staff in
tribute to the forces of the Army Artillery.

076   Ridgway, Matthew B. and Walter R. Winton, Jr.
"Troop Leadership at the Operational Level" Military
Review 70 (April 1990) 57-68.

Edited version of a seminar lecture delivered 9 May
1984, at the Command and General Staff College, dealing
with the difficulties of large ground command in Korea,
and on the large Far East level.

077   Ridgway, Matthew B.   "Troop Leadership at the
Operational Level: The Eighth Army in Korea" Address,
May 9, 1984, Command and Staff College, Ridgway papers.

Unedited version of the address (noted above)
delivered at a leadership conference.

078 Ridgway, Matthew B. "U. N. Command Offers Proposals for Settlement of Korean Armistice Issue" Department of State Bulletin (May 19, 1952) 786-788.

The text of a statement made on May 7, 1952 by Matthew B. Ridgway as Commander in Chief United Nations Command, and released from Tokyo. Primarily it placed the decision on an armistice in the hands of the communists forces, stating that the UN has made its last offer. Referring to the vital repatriations question, which was becoming symbolic of America's position, Ridgway states "We will not buy an armistice by turning over human beings for slaughter or slavery."

079 Ridgway, Matthew B. "UN Command Reports..." UN Bulletin 11 (August 1, 1951) 100.

Primarily a series of long quotes from Ridgway in which he describes the enemy withdrawal under United Nations pressures. He reports the enemy has lost over 100,000 casualties during the current military offensive.

080 Ridgway, Matthew B. "U. N. Commander Praises Work of Civilian Specialists" Department of State Bulletin 25 (August 26, 1951) 305-306.

In a letter written to the Secretary-General of the United Nations on August 1, 1951, General Ridgway thanks the civilian specialists provided by the numerous agencies of the United Nations for their help in Korea. He enumerates this help in his letter which is printed in its entirety.

081 Ridgway Matthew B. "Warning of Red Trickery" US News 31 (August 17, 1951) 20-22.

In this interview Ridgway warns he sees no peaceful intent in the Reds, and argues against any let down of supplies to the troops.

082 Ridgway, Matthew B. "What Are We Fighting For?" Canadian Army Journal 10 (March 1951) 68-69.

The text of the speech Ridgway made on assuming command of the Eighth Army in Korea in December of 1950, provided with a preface for the Canadian reader.

GENERAL BIOGRAPHICAL INFORMATION

BOOKS

083   Galloway, K. Bruce and Robert Bowie Johnson, Jr. West Point: America's Power Fraternity. New York: Simon and Schuster, 1973.
    Listed as a "definitive examination of the West Point Power Fraternity" it quotes Ridgway on several occasions, some insightful as to his period at West Point.   On teaching at the Point (78-79), on military quarters (36-37), evaluating Walker in Korea (174-191), on the canal zone (199), on the good life (203), and service in Nicaragua (273-74).

084   Glyn, Patrick.   Closing Pandora's Box. New York: Harper Collins, 1992. 144 pages, photographs.
    A brief, but interesting, account of the military in world politics including Ridgway's rather important role.

ARTICLES

085   Review of The Korean War. Collins, George W. "Korea in Retrospect" Air University Quarterly Review 20 (1968) 113-117.
    A review essay of The Korean War by Matthew Ridgway is favorable to both the book and to Ridgway's contribution to the Korean War.

086   Review of Soldier.   Allison, John M. "The Problem of Unlimited Warfare" Saturday Review (November 4, 1967) 43.
    In-depth review of Ridgway's book.   Very positive to both Ridgway and United Nation involvement.

087   Review of Soldier.   Harrison, Gordon A.   "General in the Atomic Age" Saturday Review 39 (April 14, 1956) 29.
    A long review of Ridgway's book.   Makes the case for keeping the Joint Chiefs of Staff free from any party expedience or bureaucracy.

088   Review of <u>Soldier</u>.   Maloff, Saul.   "A Soldier Speaks Up" <u>Newsweek</u> (November 20, 1967) 112.
    In-depth review of Ridgway's book. Links Korea to Vietnam and identifies Ridgway's desire to have us win there.

089 Review of <u>Soldier</u>. Moffett, Hugh.   "Plain Talk on Korea by the Boss" <u>Life</u> (November 17, 1967)
    Review essay of Ridgway's book.   In the review Ridgway is credited with settling a lot of old scores.

090 Review of <u>Soldier</u>. Phillips, T. R. "Soldier to be Proud of" <u>Reporter</u> 14 (May 31, 1956) 45-46.
    A review of Ridgway's book <u>Soldier</u>. This in-depth commentary is about Ridgway the soldier who has written an interesting book. One which reflects his devotion to duty as well as his courage and determination. Ridgway's strongest criticism is directed toward Secretary of Defense Wilson. Of Ridgway's efforts at NATO, Phillips quotes two Frenchmen who say: "Perhaps Ridgway was good for us, but we could not stand another like him."

091 Alberts, Robert C. "Profile of a Soldier: Matthew B. Ridgway" <u>American Heritage</u> 27:2 (February 1976) 5-7, 73-82.
    Using interviews the author traces the career of Matthew Ridgway, selected to replace MacArthur in April of 1951.   Ridgway went on to assume command of NATO Forces and became Chief of Staff.

092   Baker, Everett Moore.   "Thank God for Families!" <u>Parents</u> 26 (August 1951) 26.
    Listed in periodical works under Ridgway, it is a portrait of Ridgway and his family, with the following caption: "The Ridgways are reunited in the East where the General is in command. Matthew Jr.'s parents are bringing him up with <u>Parents' Magazine</u>'s help." There is no reference in the article.

093 Colby, Elbridge. "Sense of High Calling" _America_
(May 5, 1956).
    Considers the life of Ridgway, as portrayed in
Soldier, and recognizes the character and devotion of
this leader with strong religious convictions.

094 Cook, J. Aaron. "Ridgway--The Legend" _Static Line_
(March 1983).
    Brief article, written late in the General's life,
trying to capture the Ridgway tradition in a few words.

095 Erskin, Helen Worden. "Pretty Penny Ridgway -- The
General's Lady" _Colliers_ (May 16, 1953).
    While it sounds like a gossip column, this
interesting account gives some considerable insight into
Ridgway's life as NATO commander, and his (as well as
her) responsibilities. Provides some helpful personal
looks at the General that cannot be found elsewhere.

096 Graebner, Norman A. "Matthew B. Ridgway: Cold War
Statesman" _John Briggs Cincinnati Lectures in Military
Leadership and Command 1987_.   Lexington, Virginia:
Virginia Military Institute, 1987. 157-184.
    A short analysis of Ridgway's dual role as military
and political leader at a time when he was involved in
tough hot and cold wars.

097 Harper, Mr. "The General's Grenade" _Harper's
Magazine_ 203 (September 1951) 101-102.
    Addresses the grenades carried by General Matthew
Ridgway. The author identifies it as his trademark. In
a tongue-in-cheek account the author suggests that
perhaps it was not his decision, but part of the
tendency of American generals in the Korean War to model
their uniforms on those of the enemy.

098 "Hither and Yon" _Time_ 57 (May 6, 1951) 50.
    While waiting news of his fourth star, Ridgway
greets his wife and son at the Tokyo airport.

099 "Honored" _Newsweek_ 46 (July 11, 1955) 35.
    Ridgway receives his third oak-leaf cluster for his
Distinguished Service Medal, June 29, 1955.

100   Janowitz, Morris.   "Military Career Patterns and the Military Mind" Weigley, Russell (editor).   <u>The American Military: Readings in the History of the Military in American Society</u>.   Reading, Massachusetts: Addison-Wesley Publishing Company, 1969. Chapter 17.

Janowitz looks at what he considers the various career formulas and the formation of the military mind. In this chapter he presents an excellent career analysis of Ridgway as well as others.

101   Lempke, Duane A.   "Ridgway's Leadership Legacy" <u>Military Review</u> 68 (November 1988) 69-75.

In this brief sketch the author not only chronicles Ridgway's role in the most challenging operations of World War II and Korea, but also credits him with making a lasting imprint on leadership in the US Army. Based on a personal interview taken when the General was in his 70s.

102   "Matthew Bunker Ridgway" <u>Current Biography 1947.</u> Anna Rothe (editor).   New York: H. W. Wilson and Company.

In light of the fact there is no good biography of Ridgway, this account -- excellent up to 1947 -- is a good source for information on the General and his early career. 540-542.

103   McHenry, Robert (editor).   <u>Webster's American Military Biographies</u>.   Springfield, Massachusetts: Merriam, 1978.

Contains good essays on major figures in the Korean War, including Generals Matthew Ridgway, MacArthur, Clark and Collins.

104   Samuels, Gertrude.   "Ridgway: Three Views of a Soldier" <u>New York Times Sunday Magazine</u>. (April 22, 1951).

This <u>New York Times Magazine</u> writer worked with Ridgway in Korea and interviewed him for this study of the General as Far East Commander. A man she finds is tough and astute but also warm-hearted in his human relations.

105   Schumach, Murray.   "The Education of Matthew Ridgway" New York Times Sunday Magazine. (May 4, 1952). This in-depth report is concerned with Ridgway's growing political experience as this "master of the hot war, has taken over military control of the greatest 'cold war' in history". Describes the General's workday as well as the type of concerns he must face daily.

106 Spiller, Roger J. (editor). Dictionary of American Military Biography. Volume 3. Westport, Connecticut: Greenwood, 1984.
    Contains about thirty brief, but helpful, accounts of military leaders who served in World War II and Korea, including Ridgway. 909-913.

107 Who Was Who in American History -- The Military. Chicago: Marquis Who's Who, 1975.
    Contains more than 140 brief sketches of military leaders who were in World War II and Korea, including Matthew B. Ridgway.

MEMOIRS: CIVILIAN LEADERS AND MILITARY COMMANDERS

BOOKS

108 Abramson, Rudy. The Life of W. Averell Harriman, 1891-1986. New York: William Morrow and Company, 1992.
    This biography of a leading ambassador and counsel to presidents only mentions Ridgway as part of the larger picture, but makes some interesting comments on Ridgway both in relation to the Korean War and in the concerns over NATO. 450-453, 459, 608.

109 Acheson, Dean. The Korean War. New York: W. W. Norton and Company, 1971.   153 pages, index, photographs, maps.
    This work, by the US Secretary of State during the Korean War, comes as a defense of the administration's policies in Korea. He is very critical of MacArthur and supports the decision to assign Ridgway first to Eighth Army and then as MacArthur's replacement.

110   Acheson, Dean.   <u>Present at the Creation: My Years at the State Department</u>.   New York: W. W. Norton & Company, 1969.

The autobiography of US Secretary of State, who was in State from 1941 to 1953 and a major decision maker concerning policy in World War II and in Korea. Considered a major source of political and diplomatic insights but deals, as well, with the political underpinnings of the military: MacArthur and Ridgway in particular.

111   Blumenson, Martin.   <u>Mark Clark: The Last of Great World War II Commanders</u>.   New York: Congdon, 1984.

This very appreciative biography follows Clark's career through Europe (where he was associated with Ridgway) and in Korea where he served under Ridgway. It focuses on the World War II period and is supportive of Clark and the general command structure.

112   Bradley, Omar N. and Clay Blair.   <u>A General's Life: An Autobiography of General of the Army Omar N. Bradley</u>. New York: Simon and Schuster, 1983.

This is the life of General Bradley as first division commander of the 82nd Airborne Division, field commander in North Africa, of the American troops (nearly 1.3 million) at D-day, later as head of the VA, Chief of Staff, Chairman of the Joint Chiefs, and advisor to Truman over Korea. During all of this time Bradley is a friend and military mentor to Ridgway who, in many cases, is following close behind in assignments. Critical of both MacArthur and Secretary of Defense Johnson. The mentions of Ridgway are too numerous to list but it has an excellent index.

113   Bradley, Omar N. <u>A Soldier's Story</u>. New York: Henry Holt and Company, 1951.   618 pages, index, photographs, maps.

This autobiography of Bradley, Ridgway's superior on several occasions, contains numerous indexed references to Ridgway. It includes the much confused story of Ridgway's gift to Bradley of Field Marshall Model's Mercedes-Benz staff car.   529.

114   Clark, Mark W. Calculated Risk. New York: Harper and Brothers, Publishers, 1950.   500 pages, index, photographs, maps.
      This is primarily a story of Clark's military life, a   life   which   coincides   with   Ridgway   on   numerous occasions.   However it is of most interest to Ridgway scholars because of his dealing with the 1943 decisions about the use of the 82nd Airborne in and around the plains of Naples during the Italian campaign.   179, 202-203, 208, 211-236.

115   Clark, Mark W. From the Danube to the Yalu. New York: Harpers and Brothers, 1954. 369 pages, index, photographs, maps.
      An autobiography of one of Ridgway's commanders and replacement.   Concerns Ridgway both in the armistice talks; "Summary of Main United Nations Committee and Communists   Proposals   Submitted   During   Armistice Meetings,   April   and   May   1953";   and   Ridgway's authorization to use force in Koje-do Island mutiny.

116 Clifford, Clark with Richard Holbrooke.   Counsel to the President: A Memoir.   New York: Anchor Books, Doubleday, 1991.
      This is primary the memoirs of Clark Clifford who was   political   counsel   to   Presidents   Truman   and Eisenhower. However, it covers a significant period of Ridgway's career not covered elsewhere.   Ridgway as chief of staff, and in association with General Zwicker, stood up to Joe McCarthy's effort to taint the military with his tar brush of communism, and effectively stopped the attack at that point. 290-293, 504, 608.

117   Collins,   J.   Lawton.   Lightning   Joe: An Autobiography. Baton Rouge, Louisiana: Louisiana State University Press, 1979. 462 pages, photographs.
      A recount of his experiences in war and peace; primarily during World War II, and one chapter on those years   (1949-1953)   when   he   served   as   chief   of   staff, including Ridgway who served as his deputy chief of staff. 198-211, 283-296, 374-375.

118 Collins, J. Lawton. <u>War in Peacetime: The History and Lessons of Korea</u>. Boston: Houghton Mifflin, 1969. viii, 416 pages, index, photographs, maps.

General Collins, who served in Europe with Ridgway, and under whom, as chief of staff, Ridgway served, has written an able account of the efforts, and failures of the Korean War period. His insights and comments based on his experience with Ridgway, both as a commander and as a planner, is highly significant. Ridgway's role is well indexed.

119 MacArthur, Douglas A. <u>Reminiscences</u>. New York: McGraw Hill, 1964.

Little of what one would expect from the personal "reminiscences" of a man who was a military leader, and political force, for nearly 60 years. Much of it is reprinted from other sources. Contains some scattered materials about Ridgway, but everything is made to look subservient to MacArthur.

120 Manchester, William. <u>American Caesar: Douglas MacArthur 1880-1964</u>. New York: Dell Publishing Co., 1978. 960 pages, index, maps, bibliography.

Primarily a biography of MacArthur but contains some interesting and seemingly neutral commentary on Ridgway in Korea. Manchester, while not totally supportive makes the point that MacArthur was militarily and politically "misunderstood".

121 Oliver, Robert T. <u>Syngman Rhee: The Man Behind the Myth</u>. New York: Dodd Mead and Company, 1954. 380 pages, index, appendix.

This biography, written by a man who knew and worked with Rhee, is a very sensitive account of the turbulent years of Rhee's life, and deals in considerable depth with the years identified as the war for Korean independence. This material has some short, but good accounts of meetings with Ridgway, and a picture of the General with Rhee.

122   Smith, Robert.   MacArthur in Korea: The Naked
Emperor. New York: Simon & Schuster, 1982. 256 pages,
index, photographs, maps, bibliography.
    In this assessment of MacArthur's role in Korea
Smith is willing to admit to MacArthur's skills as an
advocate of action, as well as a very courageous
soldier, but stops there. He sees MacArthur as a
demigod whose own inability to listen and take criticism
pushed him into a position that was politically
misinformed and militarily outdated. In this account we
learn of MacArthur's attitude concerning Ridgway (rated
him at the bottom of a list of ten commanders) and how
Ridgway fit into the General's plans.

123   Smith, Walter Bedell.   Eisenhower's Six Great
Decisions: Europe 1944-1945. New York: Longmans, Green,
1956.
    Bedell Smith was Eisenhower's chief of staff from
September 1942 until victory. He was responsible for
most of the planning for the eventual victory, and an
influential participator in supporting Ridgway and the
use/misuse of the 82nd Airborne during World War II
particularly in Sicily.

124   Taylor, Maxwell D.   Swords and Plowshares.   New
York: W. W. Norton & Co., Inc., 1972. 434 pages, index,
photographs, maps.
    General Maxwell D. Taylor followed the same line of
career development and military command as did Ridgway,
rising even higher to be the adviser to presidents.
Much of his military career followed Ridgway, who was
often his immediate commander, and General Taylor has a
lot to say about this colleague. Of particular
significance is one of the few accounts of Ridgway's
disagreement with MacArthur: the obvious displeasure
when MacArthur claimed credit for Operation Killer, and
basic disagreements about the way the Korean War should
have been fought. General Ridgway is indexed carefully
and can be found throughout this very insightful account
of a distinguished soldier.

125   Taylor, Maxwell D.   The Uncertain Trumpet.   New York: Harper, 1959.

A personal narrative, by General Taylor, who was commander of the eighth army and army chief of staff. It was Taylor, as well as Ridgway, who seemed to have learned the lessons of Korea, and who was to support Ridgway's concern for ground troop preparation. It is openly critical of both United States policy, and the execution of the Korean War.

126 Truman, Harry S. Memoirs, Volume 2, Years of Trial and Hope. Garden City, New York: Doubleday and Company, 1956.

Truman was, of course, in the middle of the conflict both in and about Korea. As Commander-in-Chief his approval was necessary for almost any policy change. While the armistice was a military rather than a political endeavor, his involvement is obvious. He discusses Ridgway as MacArthur's replacement (454-463) and on several other occasions which are well indexed.

THE WORLD WAR YEARS: 1917-1948

Pre-World War II Years

127   Sligh, Robert Bruce. The National Guard and National Defense. New York: Praeger, 1992. 187 pages, index, bibliography.

Contains a very brief but important discussion of Ridgway's fear of Nazi Germany's aggression in South America.   Ridgway believed that the US lacked the resources necessary to defend the Western Hemisphere and to move in both Europe and Asia.   He pushed the mobilization of the National Guard. 70-72.

Applicable General Histories of World War II

BOOKS

128   Cline, Ray S. United States Army in World War II: The War Department, Washington Command Post: The Operations Division. Washington, DC: Office of the Chief of Military History, Department of the Army, 1951.
Deals with then Colonel Ridgway in the War Plans, Latin American Section, and his role in questions of psychological warfare, and the release of decoded Japanese messages (called "Magic"). Brief but informative concerning both his role and style as a staff and planning member. 82-84.

129   Eisenhower, Dwight D. Report by the Supreme Commander to the Combined Chiefs of Staff on the Operations in Europe of the Allied Expeditionary Forces, 6 June 1944 to 8 May 1945. Washington, DC: Government Printing Office, 1946. 123 pages.
The official report of the commander-in-chief in Europe and essential for an understanding of Ridgway's role in World War II.

130   Eisenhower, John S. D. The Bitter Woods. New York: G. P. Putnam's Sons, 1969. 505 pages, index, photographs, maps.
Ridgway was a part of the crisis that shook the Western Coalition when Hitler's forces provided a surprise defense at the Ardennes.

131   Harrison, Gordon A. US Army in World War II, European Theater of Operations: Cross Channel Attack. Volume 1. Washington, DC: Office of the Chief of Military History, Department of the Army, 1951.
This official history of the invasion period contains some brief but informative accounts of Ridgway. Deals with proposed changes in the organization of the airborne unit pushed by Ridgway, and an analysis of Ridgway's performance with the 82nd Airborne Division during and after the D-day invasion. 184-185, 289-291, 344-346, 398-406.

132 Keegan, John. <u>Six Armies in Normandy</u>. New York: Viking Press, 1982. 365 pages, index, maps.
     A good and fair retelling of the D-day story. See particularly Chapter Two, and Keegan's analysis of the "All American Screaming Eagles". 69-114.

133 Matloff, Maurice and Edwin M. Snell. <u>US Army in World War II, The War Department: Strategic Planning for Coalition Warfare, 1941-1942</u>. Volume 9. Washington DC: Office of the Chief of Military History, 1953.
     Deals with the vital plans for combining the allied forces in the emerging battle plan for World War II, compiled while Ridgway was still in war planning. 13, 104, 112.

134 Perret, Geoffrey. <u>There's A War to be Won: The United States Army in World War II</u>. New York: Random House, 1991. 626 pages, index, photographs, maps.
     This account of World War II is not so much about the war as about the army, and is very helpful to provide an understanding of what was going on beyond the usual list of battles and commanders. Ridgway figures predominately in the early envisioning of airborne warfare. Commentary about him is easily located in the large index.

135 Pogue, Forrest. <u>The Supreme Command</u>. Washington, DC: Office of the Chief of Military History, 1954. 607 pages, index, photographs, maps, bibliography, and appendix.
     A history of coalition warfare, focused on the agency as well as the commander of the Supreme Command. Pogue deals with the decisions and compromises which made a united action possible in Korea, including some which directly affected Ridgway.

136 Snyder, Louis L. <u>Historical Guide to World War II</u>. Westport, Connecticut: Greenwood Press, 1982. 838 pages.
     Discusses Ridgway in a rather wide variety of World War II events, found primarily between pages 505 and 586.

137 Watson, Mark Skinner. <u>US Army in World War II, The War Department</u>. Volume 1. Washington, DC: Office of the Chief of Military History, 1950.

Most interesting for Ridgway scholars in that it includes Ridgway's contributions at the office of War Planning, which led to the very significant decision on fighting fronts. The National Strategic Decisions, Memo (WPD 4175-4177) issued on the 22nd of May 1940 determines that American efforts (eventually allied efforts) had to concentrate on the Western Hemisphere. And, in order to accomplish this concentration the United States could tolerate the loss of Wake, Guam and even the Philippines in a waiting game. This was the down side of plan "Grange" for victory against Japan. 105.

82nd and General Airborne Operations

BOOKS

138 Blair, Clay. <u>Ridgway's Paratroopers: The American Airborne in World War II</u>. Garden City, New York: The Dial Press, 1985. 588 pages, index, photographs, maps.

By far the best account of the life and times of General Ridgway. Using the vast Ridgway papers, interviews with the General and members of his close military staff, as well as the papers of associated and allied commanders, Blair has provided an almost daily account of the World War II career of this airborne commander. Some initial information is provided concerning his early military career, as well as occasional comments on his personal life, but it is primarily directed to his World War II contributions as commander of the 82nd Airborne Division and the Eighteenth Airborne Corps in Europe. An excellent and well documented work. His footnotes alone are worth the reading.

139 Dawson, W. Forrest. _Saga of the All-American (82nd Airborne Division)_. Privately printed. n.d.
     As founding commander and leader in airborne warfare General Ridgway is featured at intervals throughout this "year book" effort. Has some unusual perspectives but is difficult to use and it is primarily illustration with no index or comments.

140 Gavin, James M. _On To Berlin_. New York: The Viking Press, 1978. 336 pages, index, photographs, maps.
     The story of the 82nd Airborne Division after General Gavin assumed command on Ridgway's promotion. Much of the story, however, focuses on Ridgway who was the Eighteenth Airborne Corps commander. It is a detailed and very supportive account of Ridgway both as a commander and as a tactician of airborne combat. Interesting but opinionated. 41-284.

141   Hoyt, Edwin P. _Airborne: The History of The American Parachute Forces_. New York: Stein and Day, Publishers, 1979. 228 pages, index, photographs, maps.
     This popular military historian provides some interesting discussion of the drop at Gela, with particular reference to the drop near Paestum. Well-indexed. 28-34, 36-44, 78-79, 166-167.

142 Strawson, John. _The Battle for the Ardennes_. New York: Charles Scribner's Sons, 1972. 212 pages, index, photographs, maps.
     Ridgway's Eighteenth Airborne Corps, especially the 101st Airborne Division, was committed at Bastogne, and a part of the primary confusion of the counter-attack.

143 Thompson, Leroy. _The All Americans: The 82nd Airborne_. New York: A David & Charles Military Book, 1988. 192 pages, index, photographs.
     While primarily a popular/photographic history of the 82nd, it does have both commentary and pictorial coverage of Ridgway while he was the Division Commander in Sicily (26-40), Italy (44-46), Normandy (59-61) and the Ardennes (63, 69, 76-77).

ARTICLES

144 Mason, Charles W. "The 82nd Division Under Ridgway"
Unpublished article in Box 5, Ridgway Papers, USAMHI.
     Short and perhaps unnecessarily detailed account of
Ridgway's contribution in the development of the
division and airborne tactics.

Airborne Histories and Operations

BOOKS

145 Breuer, William B. Geronimo! American Paratroopers
in World War II. New York: St. Martin's Press, 1989.
622 pages, index, maps.
     Using the recollections of 562 former paratroopers,
the author recreates airborne battles throughout Europe,
the Mediterranean and Asia. Deals with Ridgway at
Ardennes (376-461), Avalanche (115-151), Husky (58-92),
Market Garden (326-329), Overlord (182-257), and Varsity
(557-558).

146 Dank, Milton. The Glider Gang. Philadelphia: J. B.
Lippincott, 1977. 273 pages, index, photographs, maps.
     One of the few histories of the glider pilots of
World War II, many of whom lost their lives in landings
with the 82nd. In this work Dank takes a look at
Ridgway's successful effort to block the planned jump
into Sicily, and reports on General "Boy" Browning's
criticism of Ridgway for not accepting the plan. 70-84,
91-95, 236-37, 246.

147 Devlin, Gerard M. Paratrooper! The Saga of U. S.
Army and Marine Parachute and Glider Combat Troops
During World War II. New York: St. Martin's, 1979. 717
pages, index, photographs, maps, bibliography.
     A detailed account of the development of the
airborne division, and a careful depicting of airborne
operations during World War II. It contains a large
amount of official and anecdotal information on Ridgway

as airborne pioneer, as well as on the 82nd Airborne division and the Eighteenth Airborne Corps.   Well indexed so the reader can easily follow Ridgway's role in the European victory.

148 Flanagan, Edward M. Jr. <u>The Angels: A History of the 11th Airborne Division</u>.   Novato, California: Presidio Press, 1989. 422 pages, index, maps.
    A very brief account of the 11th Airborne. Flanagan discusses Ridgway's disillusionment after the division's failure in this joint action in Sicily, as well as concern over the role of the airborne.

149 Gavin, James M. <u>Air Assault</u>. New York: Hawthorn Books, Inc., 1969.
    Another account of World War II airborne which, because of Ridgway's close association with Gavin, necessarily includes some Ridgway materials. Most of this, however, is available in other Gavin productions.

150 Gavin, James M. <u>Airborne Warfare</u>. Washington, DC: Infantry Journal Press, 1947. 186 pages, index, photographs, maps.
    Concerned primarily with Gavin's 505th Parachute Combat Team (reinforced), and with the 82nd Division which he was later to command. It does give a good picture of Ridgway as the larger unit commander. Ridgway is mentioned throughout, and is well indexed.

151 Huston, James A. <u>Out of the Blue: U. S. Army Airborne Operations in World War II</u>. Lafayette, Indiana: Purdue University Studies, 1972. 327 pages, index.
    Ridgway featured strongly in this work on early airborne development and implementation. It includes Ridgway's July 1943 "Principles of Operation" (162-163) and is well indexed for other entries.

152 Marshall, Samuel L. A. <u>Bastogne: The First Eight
Days, US Army in Action Series</u>. Washington, DC: Infantry
Journal Press, 1946, 1991. 261 pages, photographs.
     This excellent military historian provides a good
account of the difficulties suffered at Bastogne, and
the role played by units of the XVIII Airborne Corps
serving under Ridgway.

153 Marshall, Samuel L. A.   <u>Night Drop</u>.   Boston:
Little, Brown and Company, 1962. 425 pages.
     An in-depth study of the Airborne action which
precluded the Normandy invasion. Strong support for
Ridgway's role in the development of operational
planning.

154 Tugwell, Maurice. <u>Airborne to Battle: A History
of Airborne Warfare, 1918-1971</u>. London: William Kimber,
1971. 367 pages, index, photographs, maps.
     Primarily a history of airborne warfare. Ridgway
as an early pioneer and commander of this first Airborne
Division is heavily referenced, all of which are
indexed. Perhaps the most interesting aspect is
Ridgway's comments on the use of the C-46 as a combat
drop aircraft. 274-276.

155 <u>U. S. A. Airborne 50th Anniversary</u>. Paducah,
Kentucky: Turner Publishing, 1992.
     Primarily a popular pictorial history of this
airborne service, but has value to the researcher as it
provides one of the few descriptions of "Operation
Varsity" for which Ridgway had ground command of the
First Allied Airborne Army. Primarily 62-63 but several
references in index.

156 <u>USAF Airborne Operations: World War II and Korean
War</u>. Washington, DC: USAF Historical Division, Liaison
Office: Air University, March 1962.
     Typed copy in the Command and Staff College
Library, Leavenworth, Kansas. Chapters V, VI, VIII, and
X all deal with units under Ridgway's command and make
many references to him.

157 Warren, John C. USAF Historical Studies: No. 97:
Airborne Operations In World War II, European Theater.
Washington, DC: USAF Historical Division, Research
Studies Institute, Air University, September 1956. 238
pages, ringbound, xeroxed.
     An in-depth study of the use of airborne troops,
including glider commands, during the European phase of
World War II. A valuable study of airborne in war and
of Ridgway's contribution. Ridgway is indexed and
referenced throughout. This is particularly good as a
source for First Allied Airborne Army and XVIII Airborne
Corps official records, see notes.

ARTICLES

158 Liell, William. "United States Airborne" Journal
of the United Service Institution of India 92 (April-
June 1962) 139-148.
     A brief report on the 1st Allied Airborne Army
including a discussion of Market Garden, Varsity, and
the XVIII Airborne, all of which report on Ridgway.

Military Commander: World War II

BOOKS

159 Blumenson, Martin. U. S. Army in World War II:
Salerno to Cassino. U. S. Army in World War II.
Washington, DC: Government Printing Office, 1969.
     This US Army official history deals with the
airborne participation in the Italian campaign,
providing excellent analysis of the almost daily
operation of the 82nd.

160 Blumenson, Martin. Sicily: Whose Victory. New
York, Ballentine Books, 1969. 161 pages, photographs.
     A cheap collection of photographs and narrative
which offers little new. Ridgway is discussed in the
section called Airborne Reinforcements.

161 Cole, Hugh M. U. S. Army in World War II, European Theater of Operation: Ardennes: Battle of the Bulge. Washington, DC: Department of Army, 1958, 1965. 720 pages, index, photographs, maps.
     A brief but detailed account of Ridgway while he was commander of the 82nd Division, and of Eighteenth Airborne Corps during the decisive Battle of the Bulge. Most useful to see the overall planning, and how the airborne under Ridgway fit into the execution of the plan. 305-307, 365-368.

162 Cookenden, Napier. Dropzone Normandy. New York: Charles Scribner's Sons, 1976. 304 pages, index, photographs.
     This book, written by a brigadier general, serving in the Glider Command, provides good coverage of Ridgway's role in glider use and formation. Chapters One and Five deal with Ridgway's role in the addition of a glider infantry regiment to the 82nd Airborne Division, for a more balanced command and the use of gliders during the Normandy invasion.

163 Devlin, Gerard M. Silent Wings. New York: St. Martin's Press, 1985. Index.
     One of the very few accounts of the United States Army and Marine combat glider pilots during World War II. The author seems greatly concerned with what he sees as poor planning which went into glider use, and complains about the lack of official support by Ridgway and other commanders. He admits the gliders provided less than anticipated performance. Ridgway's involvement is well indexed.

164 Farrar-Hockley, Anthony. Airborne Carpet: Operation Market Garden. London: Macdonald, 1970. 160 pages, bibliography.
     One of the few references to "Operation Linnet II" originally scheduled to be under the ground command of Ridgway. It was canceled by General Omar Bradley who decided instead to concentrate on Operation Market Garden. General references, also 30-31.

165 Galvin, John R.   Air Assault: The Development of Airmobile Warfare. New York: Hawthorne Books, Inc. 1969. 365 pages, index, maps.

A brief history of the airborne concept, Galvin relies on his own experience as he considers Ridgway's unique role, and his command use of the airborne in both World War II and Korea. Written by this once commander of the 82nd Airborne, it reflects a high regard for Ridgway. 104-110, 140-148, 238-249, 261.

166 Garland, Albert N. and Howard McGaw Smyth. U.S. Army in World War II, European Theater of Operation, Sicily and the Surrender of Italy. Washington, DC: Government Printing Office, 1965. 609 pages, index, photographs, maps.

In this official accounting of the long and complicated Sicily campaign, Ridgway's role is highlighted in several incidents, 101-102, 254-255, 498-509; and as well as an analysis of airborne tactics 175-176.

167 Hamilton, Nigel. Master of the Battlefield: Monty's War Years, 1942-1944. New York: McGraw Hill Book Company, 1983. 863 pages, index, photographs.

The author writes a rather subjective account of the decisions as well as the planning and executions, of this famed British commander He gives in to some of Monty's assumptions, but provides some interesting comment on Ridgway and the American Airborne. 286, 385, 400-409, 416.

168 Jackson, William G. F. The Battle for Italy. New York: Harper & Row, Publishers, 1967. 372 pages, index, photographs, maps, charts.

The best single volume history available of the Italian campaign. While Jackson only mentions General Ridgway in a peripheral sense (54, 94-96) he does discuss in considerable detail Ridgway's concern over the use of Airborne forces.

169   Leckie, Robert. <u>Deliver from Evil: The Saga of
World War II</u>. New York: Harper and Row, Publishers,
1987. 998 pages, index, photographs, maps, bibliography.
    A usual consideration of World War II, primarily in
Europe, but it does have a couple of interesting
comments on Ridgway's role in the D-Day drop (681),
Operation Market Garden (yet another view 768-770) and
at the rescue attempt during the battle of the Bulge
(816-817).

170   MacDonald, Charles B. <u>A Time for Trumpets: The
Untold Story of The Battle of The Bulge</u>. New York:
William Morrow and Company, Inc., 1985. 712 pages,
index, photographs, maps, appendix (order of battle).
    An excellent study of the Battle of the Bulge from
beginning to end. Does a nice job of chronicling
Ridgway's role in the final days and in working out the
confusion brought on by the mixed and debilitating
command overlap. Well indexed.

171   MacDonald, Charles B. <u>United States Army in World
War II, The European Theater of Operations, The
Siegfreid Line Campaign</u>. Washington, DC: Office of the
Chief of Military History, Department of the Army, 1963.
670 pages, index, photographs, maps.
    This official history traces the European Command
from the breaching of the Siegfreid Line to the 9th
Army's final push to the Ruhr, and the approaches to
Dueren. It includes a detailed account of Operation
Market Garden, and the "invasion from the sky" which
deals with much of the Ridgway command. Ridgway
himself, however, is only dealt with on a limited basis.

172   Nobecourt, Jacques. <u>Hitler's Last Gamble: The
Battle of the Bulge</u>. London: Chatto & Windus, 1967. 302
pages, bibliography.
    This brief battle is little more than an incident
in a war fraught with consequences, but because of the
reverse inflicted on the Allies during such a victorious
period it has taken on gigantic proportions. General
Ridgway and the paratroopers are well considered. 168-
171, 213, 219, 225-236.

173   Powell, Geoffrey.   <u>The Devil's Birthday: The
Bridges at Arnhem, 1944</u>. New York: Franklin Watts, 1985.
275 pages, index, photographs.
      The story of Operation Market Garden.   Ridgway
material is scattered throughout and is well indexed.
Most concentrated entries occur on pages 134-136.
Interesting account of Ridgway who "effectively reduced
to an administrative officer" flew with Brereton to
watch the 101st on the first day of battle.

174   Ruppenthal, Roland G.   <u>American Forces in Action
Series: Utah Beach to Cherbourg</u>.   Washington, DC:
History Department, Department of the Army, 1984. 212
pages, index, photographs, maps.
      Deals with Ridgway as commander of the 82nd
Airborne Division astride the Merderet (30-34), and the
82nd at Ste. Mere-Eglise (61+).

175   Ryan, Cornelius.   <u>The Longest Day: June 6, 1944</u>.
New York: Simon and Schuster, Inc., 1959.
      In this popular and excellent account of the D-day
landing Ridgway and his airborne units play a
significant part.   131-135, 141-143.

176   Ryan, Cornelius.   <u>A Bridge Too Far</u>.   New York:
Simon and Schuster, Inc., 1974.   670 pages, index,
photographs, maps, bibliography.
      This carefully researched work deals with Operation
Market Garden, Montgomery's plan to break a corridor
through to the heart of Germany.   The plan called for a
series of air drops the command of which were placed in
the hands of Lieutenant General Frederick "Boy"
Browning, head of the British I Airborne Corps.   Ryan
makes a case for Browning's limitations and, especially
concerning the relief of forces held up at the bridge at
Arnhem, suggests Ridgway should have had the command.
125-130, 477-479.

177 Toland, John. <u>The Last 100 Days</u>. New York: Random
House, 1966.   622 pages, index, photographs, notes.
      This popular historian addresses Ridgway's role in
Operation Varsity in the Wesel Sector, with British 6th
and US 17th from the Eighteenth Airborne Corps.

178 Trevelyan, Raleigh. Rome '44: The Battle for the Eternal City. New York: Viking, 1981. 366 pages, photographs.
     A not so well told tale of some of the harshest fighting during World War II.

179 Utah Beach to Cherbourg, 6 June - 27 June, 1944. Washington, DC: Government Printing Office, 1948. 213 pages.
     An excellent account of invasion planning and execution. Includes some Ridgway materials which are well indexed, but is overshadowed by Warren's Airborne Operations In World War II, European Theater.

180 Weigley, Russell Frank. Eisenhower's Lieutenants: The Campaign for France and Germany, 1944-1945. Bloomington: Indiana University Press, 1981. 800 pages, index, photographs, maps.
     Some insights into Ridgway's disagreement with General "Boy" Browning (290-293) and General Montgomery (546-548).

181 Whiting, Charles. Death of a Division. New York: Stein and Day Publishers, 1981. 162 pages, index, photographs, maps.
     A survey of struggles of the 106th Infantry Division. Contains a clear and concise story of Ridgway's role in working out the command confusion between General Hasbrouck and General Jones, and the eventual retreat of the 106th. 135-144.

                         ARTICLES

182 "Ridgway" Time 40 (April 2, 1945) 27-29.
     A short, highly praiseworthy, description of Ridgway, describing his appointment as XVIII Airborne Corps commander as the real punch of Brereton's First Allied Airborne Army. Rates Ridgway as the world's number one active airborne commander, seeing him as the master tactician of airborne warfare.

KOREA: 1948-1953

Between the Wars

BOOKS

183   Detzer, David.   Thunder of Captains: The Short Summer in 1950.   New York: Thomas Y. Crowell Company, 1977. 243 pages, index.
     An excellent study of the two weeks during which American involvement in Korea was argued and determined. Brief but interesting indications of Ridgway's early knowledge (116) and programming and planning of equipment involvement (168).

184   Gelb, Leslie H. with Richard K. Betts.   The Irony of Vietnam: The System Worked.   Washington, DC: The Brookings Institute, 1979. 387 pages, index.
     According to Gelb, the foreign policy failed but the decision-making system worked and it worked as it was designed to do.   Considers Ridgway's role in the 1953 decision not to bomb China if China interfered at Dien Bien Phu, his opposition to intervention in 1954, his opposition to escalation in 1966, and his role in preventing the invasion of North Vietnam during the Johnson administration.   Well indexed.

185   Graebner, Norman A. (editor).   The National Security: Its Theory and Practice 1945-1960.   New York: Oxford University Press, 1986. 316 pages, index.
     A series of essays given at West Point on national security policies under Truman and Eisenhower.   Presents Ridgway's case -- US is selling out to big weapons at the cost of an adequate ground force -- from several perspectives (65, 69, 276-277); presidential responses to Ridgway's position (208); Ridgway's intervention against a "preventive war" with Russia in 1945 (146-147); and military control of SAC targets (149, 202-203).

General Histories of the Korean War

BOOKS

186   Berger, Carl.   The Korean Knot: A Military
Political History.   Philadelphia: University   of
Pennsylvania, 1957, 1965, 1968. 255 pages, index.
     Rare history which covers the political events of
both the causes and the war itself. Excellent overview,
but limited in both scope and depth. Deals with the
MacArthur dismissal and Ridgway replacement with amazing
objectivity.   Particularly useful is Chapter 11 "The
Frustrating Negotiations."

187 Blair, Clay. The Forgotten War: America in Korea
1950-1953. New York: Times Books, 1987.
     An excellent, well researched, and documented
history of the War.   Because of Blair's interest in
Ridgway the general gets an unusually good accounting in
this one volume history.   One of the best to see
Ridgway's command structure and personal character
within the larger picture.

188   Field, James A. Jr. History of United States Naval
Operations: Korea. Washington DC: Government Printing
Office, 1962.   499 pages, index, photographs, maps.
     A good single volume history of the primarily
unknown naval aspects of the Korean War.   Numerous
references to Ridgway and his use of naval gunfire,
primarily 308-309, 421-424, and indexed by subject.

189   Gosfield, Frank and Bernhardt J. Hurwood. Korea:
Land of the 38th Parallel. New York: Parents' Magazine
Press, 1969. 254 pages, index.
     Discusses the political impact in Korea of
Ridgway's appointment as commander of Eighth Army.
Ridgway was not only able to revitalize the troops but
carried on the policies of MacArthur even after
MacArthur was wavering. See especially 116-120.

190   Goulden, Joseph C. <u>Korea: The Untold Story of the War</u>. New York: McGraw, 1982.
    This is a good standard history with little unique about its view, but it is well written and informative. Primarily a re-working of official accounts, this author sides with, and is strongly supportive of MacArthur, with surprising little support of Ridgway.

191   Hastings, Max. <u>The Korean War</u>. New York: Simon and Schuster, 1987.   389 pages, photographs, maps, bibliography.
    Hastings, a well respected British military historian, takes a good look at the Korean War, recounting the personal experience of the individual soldiers, and the strategies and politics of the leadership.   He covers Ridgway in the course of this discussion, giving the reader the insights of both a careful historian, and an observer from the British point of view, a view which comes across most favorably. Ridgway's contribution well indexed.

192   Leckie, Robert. <u>The Wars of America</u>. New York: Harper Collins Publisher, 1992. 1281 pages, index.
    A general survey of the wars which involved American troops.   Of particular interest is part nine "The Korean War" but Ridgway is indexed, and discussed 898-902, 904-907, 910-918.   Puts the Korean War in the stream of military involvement.

193   Middleton, Harry J.   <u>The Compact History of the Korean War</u>. New York: Hawthorn Books, Inc., 1965.   255 pages, index, maps, appendix.
    This journalist and professional documentarian has written an easily readable, short, and negative history of the Korean War.   The book is wary of both US and UN policies and their ability to fight. The book, however, is accepting of Ridgway and includes an interesting comparison between what he considers two dramatic personalities; Ridgway and MacArthur.   Especially 160-219.

194 The Ministry of National Defense, The Republic of
Korea. The History of the United Nations Forces in the
Korean War. 5 volumes. Seoul: Ministry of National
Defense, 1972-1974. Index, photographs, maps.
     A totally subjective history of the "three years'
fratricidal tragedy". It seems designed to excuse the
excesses of the war, but it does acknowledge with praise
the contribution of the twenty-one united nations
representatives involved in the conflict, and draw
attention to the continuing menace of the communists
view. Does provide the South Korean point of view on
the United Nations forces, and on leadership including
General Ridgway.

195 Mossman, Billy C. The United States Army in the
Korean War: Ebb and Flow, November 1950 -- July 1951.
Washington, DC: Center of Military History, United
States Army, 1990. 551 pages, index, photographs, maps.
     This excellent book, one in the official series on
the Korean War, begins with the successful but
increasingly dangerous United Nations drive toward the
Yalu river and follows the retreat of Tenth Corps and
Eighth Army across the frozen wastes of North Korea. It
is perhaps the most complete and well documented
official account of Ridgway as the military commander,
and of his contribution to whatever limited victory was
possible in the Korean War. An absolute essential for
any one studying Ridgway.

196 Rees, David. Korea: The Limited War. New York:
St. Martin's Press, 1964.   511 pages, index, maps,
appendix.
     A British author with an objective look, he
concentrates on the events leading up to the war; the
decision to stand and fight, and the early context of
containment policy. Deals with the political as well as
the military aspects of the war. Ridgway is considered
under several topics in the index, but most important
are his tactics in the winter of 1950. 186, 202, 208.

197 Rees, David (editor). The Korean War: Its History
and Tactics. New York: Crescent, 1984. Photographs.
    Good single volume of the military aspects of the
war. Best treatment of policy in relation to military
operations. Considers "American involvement in Korea,
the greatest act in recent American history".
Considerable coverage of Ridgway's contribution to both
history and tactics.

198 Schnabel, James F. United States Army in the
Korean War: The First Year. Washington, DC: Office of
the Chief of Military History, United States Army, 1972.
Index, photographs, maps.
    This essential work on the early period of the
Korean War is full of Ridgway materials and is an
excellent resource. It has a good index and Ridgway can
be found throughout subject headings. 305-314.

199 Spurr, Russell. Enter the Dragon: China's
Undeclared War Against the U. S. in Korea, 1950-1951.
New York: New Market Press, 1988. 335 pages, index,
photographs.
    Ridgway is discussed in several places and is well
indexed. Spurr considers Ridgway to be one of the most
underrated American generals and provides a strong
affirmation of Ridgway's revitalizing US troops, but
also the vitalization of ROK troops which led to the
halting of the Chinese drive South. 309-316.

200 Stokesbury, James L. A Short History of the Korean
War. New York: Quill, William Morrow, 1988. 276 pages,
index, maps.
    This volume, one in a series of "Short Histories"
is well done. The tone of this work is the
inevitability of our involvement in Korea. It is
included here because of its simple but extensive
understanding of Ridgway's role in Korea both as the
commander of Eighth Army and in the Far East Command.
This role is well indexed.

201 Stone, Isidor F. The Hidden History of the Korean War. New York: Monthly Review Press, 1952. 364 pages, index, references.
      This still remains one of the more controversial works dealing with the Korean War. Stone, a well known liberal journalist introduces the US-ROK conspiracy, placing much of the blame for the war on the US. Excellent overview of the period in which Ridgway served.

202 Toland, John. In Mortal Combat: 1950-1953. New York: William Morrow and Company, 1991. 624 pages, index, photographs, maps.
      Excellent, if somewhat subjective account of the war. Toland's analysis has the advantage of his access to the records of Chinese Communist Forces. It is weakened by his effort to recapture dialogue and describe events. Ridgway throughout is well indexed.

203 Weigley, Russell Frank. History of the United States Army. New York: The Macmillan Company, 1967. 688 pages, photographs, maps, notes.
      An interesting history of the development and organization of the army, which carries an account of Ridgway and the relationship between Ridgway, MacArthur, and the Joint Chiefs of Staff (518-526). Ridgway played this unique role as war planner and area commander. Ridgway as an alternative point of view for the campaign against the Chinese Communist Forces (553, 645n).

204 Whelan, Richard. Drawing the Line: The Korean War, 1950-1953. New York: Little Brown, 1990. 428 pages, index, maps, bibliography.
      This work addresses "why World War III was risked to save an undemocratic republic" His answers are more political and descriptive than they are analytical but he gives some initial understanding. He deals with Ridgway on several occasions, with particular interest provided in his discussion of the "paralysis" of the armistice talks in January of 1952.

ARTICLES

205   Baya, G. Emery.   "Army Organization Act of 1950"
Army Information Digest   5:8 (1950) 28-37.
     This reflects the organization of the army as it
operated throughout the war.   Signed into law by
President Truman just three days after the North Korean
invasion,   it   consolidated   several   previous
organizational laws.

206   Greenfield, Kent Roberts.   "Origins of the Army
Ground Forces: General Headquarters, United States Army,
1940-1954" U. S. Army in World War II: The Organization
of Ground Combat Troops. Greenfield, Kent Roberts,
Robert R. Palmer and Bell I. Wiley, (editors).
Washington, DC: Government Printing Office, 1947.
     This statement includes the role of airborne troops
as Ridgway was to command them.

207   "United States Far East Command, History of the
North Korean Army"   Tokyo: G-2   Section,   1952.
Manuscript.
     An attempt to trace the origins, the table of
organization and equipment, as well as the political
force behind the North Korean People's Army.

Korean Commander: Eighth Army/Far East

BOOKS

208   Alexander, Bevin.   Korea: The First War We Lost.
New York: Hippocrene Books, 1986. 558 pages, maps.
     Bevin Alexander, an Army combat historian in Korea,
was one of the first to make good use of the unpublished
narratives of combat historians, and Eighth Army Corps
command reports. More than half of the work deals with
the first year of the war, and there are some areas that
could use editorial softening, but his research is
excellent. He makes the charge that the United States,
with the aid of the United Nations, fought two wars.

One with the North Koreans which we won, and with the Chinese which we lost. He deals with the military situation with sound judgment, but comes down heavily on the high cost of misunderstanding the enemy.

209 Appleman, Roy E. Disaster in Korea: The Chinese Confront MacArthur. College Station, Texas: Texas A & M University Press, 1989. 456 pages, index, photographs, maps, notes.
     Picks up the story with the pivotal date 24 November 1950. Uses Chinese sources which makes his work very valuable, as he corrects some errors about the disaster. He challenges some of the myths about the Chinese forces, and deals openly with the "bug out" of American troops. Includes a great deal of information on Ridgway which comes from personal interviews with the General. Much of this material is very significant.

210 Appleman, Roy E. Escaping the Trap: The U. S. Army X Corps in Northeast Korea, 1950. College Station, Texas: Texas A & M University Press, 1987. 411 pages, index, photographs, maps, notes.
     Another in the excellent official histories written by this military historian. It deals with the Chinese entry into the war, the retreat, and the turn-around under Ridgway. Based on official documents and unit histories. Well indexed with numerous entries.

211 Appleman, Roy E. Ridgway Duels for Korea. College Station, Texas: Texas A & M University Press, 1990. xvi, 665 pages, photographs, maps.
     Appleman's continuing story of the Korean War. The author, perhaps the best informed historian of the War, writes from primary sources, interviews, and personal accounts. He covers the Chinese 3rd, 4th, and 5th phase offensives. He is supportive of Ridgway and recounts "wrong-way-Ridgway's" decision to attack to the North. Based on official records and interviews including Ridgway.

212 Black, Robert W. Rangers in Korea. New York: Ivy
Books, 1989. 324 pages, index, photographs.
     Discusses Ridgway's attitude toward this special
force and his refusal to use Rangers for deep
penetration into (or behind) enemy lines.

213 Burchett, Wilfred G. Again Korea. New York:
International Publishers, 1968. 188 pages, index, maps.
     This is a collection of fifteen essays on various
aspects of the Korean War, chapter four (August 22,
1952) deals with the effort by many, including Ridgway,
to contain the war while, at the same time, ignoring the
warnings of the Chinese. 29, 32, 49.

214 Cagle, Malcolm W. and Frank A. Manson. The Sea
War. Annapolis: United States Naval Institute, 1957.
554 pages, index, photographs, maps.
     Chapters one and two are helpful in understanding
Ridgway's use of naval gun fire to interdict along
coastal targets. Deals with an aspect of the war that
is poorly understood, and shows Ridgway's ability to use
the resources of combined military forces. 229-230,
372, 388, 391-414.

215 Carew, Tim. Korea: The Commonwealth at War.
London: Cassell, 1967. 307 pages, index, photographs,
appendix.
     This unofficial British history shows Ridgway's
revitalization of the troops under his command, and his
good relationship with British forces. 156-157, 169,
232, 239-240.

216 Donovan, Robert J. Nemesis: Truman and Johnson in
the Coils of War in Asia. New York: St. Martin's Press,
1984. 216 pages, index.
     The book discusses the calamitous experiences
suffered by Presidents Truman and Johnson in their
respective appearances in Asian wars. Discusses
Ridgway's early concern over the use of troops in Korea,
the turn-around of Eighth Army troops, and MacArthur's
expressions to Ridgway of his concern over Truman's
"malignant hypertension" and possible lack of rational
thought. 49, 148, 153, 165-166.

217   Eighth US Army, Military History Section.   The
First Ten Years: A Short History of the Eighth United
States Army 1944-1954.   Tokyo: Army AG Administrative
Center, 1954.
     This fairly light account of the Eighth Army which
focuses on the Korean War period.   Valuable primarily
because of Ridgway involvement which, though short, was
considered as significant to the turn-around in Korea.

218   George, Alexander L.   The Chinese Communist Army:
The Korean War and Its Aftermath.   New York: Columbia
University Press, 1967. 255, index, photographs.
     A RAND Corporation study of the Chinese Communist
Forces.   An insightful work essential to any deep
understanding of the Korean War, considers Ridgway
briefly (28-29, 163-164) and is only significant here
because it reflects the response of the Chines Communist
Forces to Ridgway's appointment as Commander of the
Eighth Army.

219   Gough, Terrence J.   US Army Mobilization and
Logistics in the Korean War.   Washington, DC: Chief of
Military History, United States Army, 1987.
     Discusses the difficulty of initial mobilization
and logistical support during the early and middle
period of the Korean War.   Despite the easy access to
Japan, supplies were both short, and hard to distribute.
Considers Ridgway's lack of respect and limited
understanding of logistical problems, though he was more
concerned than most military commanders.   98-104, 126.

220   Grey, Jeffrey.   The Commonwealth Armies and the
Korean War: An Alliance Study.   New York: Manchester
University Press, 1988.   224 pages, index, maps.
     An analysis of the role of the British Commonwealth
Forces in Korea.   Understandably he considers Ridgway as
an American as well as their commander; discusses the
American (Ridgway's) view of the British troops (84-85);
and the British view of Ridgway as MacArthur's
replacement (114-115).

221   Griffith, Samuel B. II. The Chinese People's Liberation Army. New York: McGraw Hill Book Company, 1967.   398 pages, index.

A must for an understanding of the Chinese phase of the Korean Conflict.   Quotes Ridgway both on the execution of the war and on the individual values of the Chinese Communists commanders.   149-157, 161.

222   Higgins, Trumbull.   Korea and the Fall of MacArthur.   New York: Oxford University Press, 1960.

A discussion of the unpopular nature of the war, stemming, according to Higgins, from the limited military follow-up on the US commitment.   Finds fault with MacArthur but supports Ridgway.

223 Hinshaw, Arned L. Heartbreak Ridge: Korea, 1951. New York: Praeger, 1951. 146 pages, index.

Foreword by Matthew B. Ridgway, discusses the value of Ridgway as replacement for Walker, then also as a replacement for MacArthur.   Sees the US involvement as a clear win for the United States. Forward, 20-24, 84.

224   James, Clayton D. with Anne Sharp Wells. Refighting the Last War: Command and Crisis in Korea, 1950-1953.   New York: Free Press, 1992.   400 pages, index, photographs.

A reinterpretation of the high command in Korea, it examines six major decisions, and reviews the roles, leadership ability, personalities and prejudices of the top five commanders.   Argues all were limited by perceptions learned in World War II.   Ridgway throughout, but primarily chapter three, 53-78.

225 Kahn, Ely J. Jr. The Peculiar War, Impressions of a Reporter in Korea. New York: Random, 1952. 211 pages.

Early impressions of the war by a New Yorker reporter who tries to tell what he has seen that might be of interest to the "folks" at home.   Several views of Ridgway.

226 Lee, Suk Bok. The Impact of U. S. Forces in Korea.
Washington DC: National Defense University Press, 1987.
75 pages, index, maps.
      This brief monograph by a serving officer of the
South Korean Army questions Ridgway's willingness to
stay and to fight. He suggests that Ridgway reflected
America's unnecessary fear of the Soviet Union and that
this fear continued to overly influence the way the war
was fought.

227 MacGregor, Morris J., Jr. Integration of the Armed
Forces, 1940-1965. Washington DC: Center of Military
History, 1981. 617 pages, index, photographs.
      General Ridgway was a major factor in the
integration of the military, serving not only as a
spokesperson but as the field commander who accomplished
the fact with troops under his command. Ridgway's
attitude on segregation (439); forcing the issue of
integration (442-448); integration announced July 1951
(469); and problems created by other units and
commanders (449-450).

228 Marshall, Samuel L. A. The River and the Gauntlet:
The Defeat of the Eighth Army by the Chinese Communist
Forces, November, 1950, in the Battle of the Chongchon
River, Korea. New York: Morrow, 1953.
      Based on interviews with surviving members of the
2nd and 25th Infantry Division, spotty and uneven. But
Marshall is a respected historian who has raised some
interesting questions and provided some details not
generally available elsewhere.

229 McGovern, James. To the Yalu: From the Chinese
Invasion of Korea to MacArthur's Dismissal. New York:
Morrow, 1972. 275 pages, index, photographs.
      Important account of MacArthur's decision to push
north even when it was evident the Chinese were ready to
enter the war. Ridgway is listed throughout and is well
indexed. Most significant is chapter fourteen on
MacArthur's dismissal.

230   Murphy, Edward F. Korean War Heroes. Novato, California: Presidio Press, 1992.

This interesting account of Medal of Honor winners during the Conflict includes several significant references to General Ridgway's military policy.

231   Schaller, Michael. Douglas MacArthur: The Far Eastern General. New York: Oxford University Press, 1989. 320 pages, index, maps.

A far from flattering account of Douglas MacArthur as the supreme military commander in the Far East. Has some interesting and different -- if not unique -- comments on Ridgway from his early mission to Tokyo as planner with the Joint Chiefs, his opinions of MacArthur as a commander, and of specific strategy, as well as comments on Ridgway as Eighth Army commander. 212-228.

232   Stairs, Denis. The Diplomacy of Constraint: Canada, The Korean War; and the United States. Toronto: University of Toronto, 1974.   373 pages, index, maps.

This look at Canada's contribution is primarily concerned with righting wrongs and pointing fingers. However, Ridgway comes out fairly well, both in terms of the understanding of the use of Commonwealth troops, and in recognition of the Canadian forces as units in their own right.

233   Voorhees, Melvin B. Korean Tales. New York: Simon, 1952. 209 pages, map, chronology.

A collection of essays by the Eighth Army chief censor. Deals with several military leaders including Matthew B. Ridgway as commander of the Eighth Army.

ARTICLES

234   "Award of Korean Service Medal to former Commanding General" UN Bulletin 12 (June 1, 1952) 443.

Secretary-General Trygve Lie bestowed the United Nations Korea Service Medal on Ridgway at a ceremony in the Security Council Chambers. Article outlines Ridgway's role on the United Nations Military Staff Committee during the formation of the UN, and as the first UN Military Commander.

235   "Command" Time   57 (January 1, 1951) 15.
   Announces the death of "Bulldog Walker" in a jeep accident and Ridgway's appointment as the new Eighth Army Commander. Good on both generals.

236   "Command: The Airborne Grenadier" Time   57 (March 5, 1951) 26-29.
   A rather serious look at General Ridgway who took over command of the Eighth Army in Korea. Stresses the fact Ridgway is a fighting general.

237   "Command: New SCAP" Time   57 (April 23, 1951) 35.
   Announces General Ridgway's appointment as the new Supreme Commander Allied Powers. "Oh my gosh..." he is quoted as saying.

238   "Command: Paratrooper General"   Newsweek   37 (January 8, 1951) 28.
   Ridgway, the new commander of Eighth Army is portrayed as a determined fighting man who will give his utmost to his command, and will expect the very best from others.

239   Denson, John.   "Ridgway, Will He Succeed Ike?" Colliers   129 (March 1952) 66-69.
   Despite the title, this article deals with Ridgway's performance as MacArthur's replacement. Very supportive of Ridgway and his role as supreme commander.

240   "Four Star Blunder" Time   58 (December 3, 1951) 21.
   Ridgway corrects a suggestion by General Hanley that they had documented more than 5000 cases of Red atrocities by reducing it to 365, saying Hanley exaggerated.

241   "General Ridgway Reports on Korea"   US NEWS   32 (June 6, 1952) 26.
   General Ridgway warns there is no plan in effect for the successful completion of the war in Korea.

242 Hetzel, Frederick A. and Harold L. Hitchens. "An
Interview with General Matthew B. Ridgway" Western
Pennsylvania History Magazine 65:4 (October 1982) 279-
307.
    Edited manuscript of a three-hour interview
session, 5 March, 1982. Primarily recollections of a
long military career with emphasis on his years as
commander, Eighth Army, Korea.

243 "Japan Without MacArthur" US News 30 (April 20,
1951) 23-24.
    Ridgway taking over in Japan, in addition to
overall command of American and United Nation Forces,
will move to speed up the peace settlement and self rule
for Japan.

244 "Major Policy Shift" Time 58 (September 3, 1951)
21.
    Ridgway's verbal response to the communists heats
up as American policy shifts toward the defeat of the
communists rather than containment.

245 "Matthew Ridgway Takes Command: New Boss Shakes Up
GHQ in Tokyo" Life 30 (April 30, 1951) 39.
    Ridgway arrives at the office early, calls morning
staff meetings, and generally sets the tone for a new
and more aggressive command.

246 McGregor, Greg. "Front Line General" New York
Times Sunday Magazine (March 4, 1951).
    A short but informative account of Ridgway as a
fighting general.

247 Meyers, Gilbert L. "Intervention By Chinese
Communists" Air University Quarterly Review 4:4 (1951)
89-95.
    Discusses the impact of the Chinese invasion
through March 1951. His figures seemed exaggerated and
his discussion of Ridgway's March 1951 effort in
Operation Killer paints a more optimistic picture than
seems justified.

248   Mitchener, James.   "A Tough Man for a Tough Job"
Life   32 (May 12, 1952) 103-106.
        Author James Mitchener takes a look at Ridgway as
he prepares for a new job and sees a hard working,
tough, fair-minded but determined commander.

249   Montross, Lynn.   "They Made the Sun Stand Still"
Army Combat Forces Journal   6 (December 1955) 40-41.
        An account of the role of Matthew Ridgway in Korea,
his reversal of the "retreat" mentality and his planning
of Operation Killer. Sees Ridgway as a major factor in
saving the army.

250   "New Far East Chief"   Senior Scholastic   58 (April
25, 1951) 19.
        Addressing the appointment of Matthew Ridgway, the
Scholastic describes him as "a stickler for details",
who has the devotion of his troops as well as the
respect of his superiors. Recalls an incident in which
General Ridgway, the new Far East Chief, bent over to
tie the bootlaces of a paratrooper who, because of his
heavy equipment, was unable to bend over. Uses the
story to identify the soft spoken, easy going, but well
respected infantryman who pioneered airborne tactics in
World War II. Tends to exaggeration.

251   "No End in Sight for New SCAP"   Newsweek   37 (April
30, 1951) 28.
        Ridgway faces the many facets of his new command,
all of which have significant impact, but winning the
war in Korea is still the major one. He will continue
to be involved in armistice efforts.

252   "People of the Week"   US News   30 (February 23,
1951) 37-39.
        General Ridgway "Top Soldier in Korea" expresses
his goals. "Just keep killing communists" he says,
preferring to inflict enemy casualties rather than to
gain space; the concept of "limited objective" is going
well. The article discusses the general as both a tough
and a compassionate military leader.

253   "Reports of Unified Command"   United Nations
Bulletin   10:2 (January 1, 1951) 95; 10:6 (March 15,
1951) 261; 10:8 (April 15, 1951) 392-393; 10:9 (May 1,
1951) 440-441; 10:10 (May 15, 1951) 473; 11:1 (July 1,
1951) 20; and 11:3 (August 1, 1951) 100.
        Published reports of Eighth Army commander.

254   "Ridgway and Hirohito"   Newsweek   38 (October 1,
1951) 38.
        Ridgway takes the unprecedented move of going to
the Imperial Palace to have lunch with Emperor Hirohito
and Empress Nagako.

255   "Ridgway for Walker"   Newsweek   37 (January 1,
1951) 16-17.
        Announces Ridgway as the replacement for General
Walker at Eighth Army in Korea.   A brief personal
biography of Ridgway is included.

256   "Ridgway Reports"   Newsweek   39 (June 2, 1952) 20.
        Ridgway   testified   before   the   Armed   Services
Committee who asked for a frank report on the war in
Korea.

257   Roper, Elmo and Louis Harris.   "The Press and the
Great Debate"   Saturday Review of Literature   34 (July
14, 1951) 9-10, 29-30.
        The debate over the best way to end the war in
Korea, as well as bombing Manchurian bases, ranges
between the generals and the politicians.   The debate
centers   on   the   MacArthur   dismissal   and   Ridgway's
appointment, giving Ridgway a strong vote of support.
The assumption of the article is that while Ridgway is
a more respected military leader, one can expect the
MacArthur policies in Japan to continue about as they
had been under MacArthur.

258   Schnabel, James F.   "Ridgway in Korea"   Military
Review   44:3 (1964) 3-13.
        A look at the command responsibility of Matthew
Ridgway both as Eighth Army and Far East commander.
Very   favorable   to   Ridgway,   seeing   his   ability   to
maintain morale as a prime contribution.

Armistice, Truce and POW

BOOKS

259 Bailey, Sidney D. The Korean Armistice. New York: St. Martin's Press, 1992.
Written about the dynamics of war termination, it describes the negotiations and implementation of the armistice. He considers the problems of arranging the coalition diplomacy necessary and negotiating a secure peace when dozens of nations are involved. Appendix contains significant documents which marked progress during the armistice negotiations.

260   Foot, Rosemary. A Substitute for Victory: The Politics of Peacemaking at the Korean Armistice Talks. Ithaca, New York: Cornell University Press, 1990. 237 pages, index.
Focuses on American formation of negotiating sanctions, on the relationship between military success and armistice demands, and Ridgway's effort to conduct military tactics with political goals. The relationship between daily victories and negotiations offers a different view of Ridgway's role.

261   Hermes, Walter G. The United States Army in the Korean War: Truce Tent and Fighting Front. Washington, DC: Office of the Chief of Military History, 1966. 571 pages, index, photographs, maps, bibliography.
The second in the series of official histories produced by the Chief of Military History, and an essential work for anyone studying the Korean War. It is drawn from Eighth Army combat reports, and unit journals. Ridgway is so much a part of this phase of the war in Korea, and the early stages of the armistice talks, that he accounts for a significant portion of this work. His contribution is well indexed.

262 Lawson, Don. The United States in the Korean War.
New York: Abelard-Schuman, 1964.   159 pages, index,
maps.
     This short, simple account devotes chapter seven to
a discussion of Ridgway's contribution to the outcome of
the war, and his role in the arrangement of the peace.

263 Vatcher, William H. Jr.   Panmunjom: The Story of
the Korean Military Armistice Negotiations.   New York:
Frederick A. Praeger, Inc. Publishers, 1958. 322 pages,
index, photographs, maps, chronology, appendix.
     Vatcher was the psychological warfare advisor to
the senior United Nations delegate at the Korean
armistice conference. It was written to teach Americans
how to deal with "our ruthless Communist adversaries"
but gives a pretty good picture of the armistice
procedure. Ridgway, an active part of that process, is
represented in numerous settings, all well indexed.

                         ARTICLES

264   "Agreement Reached to Hold Korean Cease-Fire
Meetings" United Nations Bulletin 11:2 (July 15, 1951)
46-49.
     General Ridgway broadcast, 29 June, 1951, an offer
to the Chinese Communist Forces to discuss a cease-fire
possibility.   This story suggests an agreement was
reached on the location for such a meeting.

265 Bacchus, Wilfred A. "The Relationship between
Combat and Peace Negotiations: Fighting While Talking in
Korea, 1951-1953" Orbis 17 (Summer 1973). 545-574.
     The author makes a case for the fact that casualty
ratios were a significant part of the agreement-making
mentality. Because the armistice was a military one
despite its political overtones, the frustrations of
restrained power played an important part in the
eventual agreement.

266 Bernstein, Barton J. "The Struggle Over the Korean Armistice: Prisoners of Repatriation?" Bruce Cumings (editor).   Child of Conflict: The Korean-American Relationship, 1943-1953.   Seattle: University of Washington Press, 1983. 261-308.
This excellent chapter from a very fine book, deals with the difficulties inherent in an armistice based, primarily, on ideological grounds. Especially when the control of the beliefs of prisoners becomes an issue, and repatriation becomes a cause. While not directly about Ridgway it covers Ridgway's involvement in this process and gives the reader considerable insight about what was wanted, how the US and the communists went about trying to get what they wanted, and how it was brought to at least a temporary conclusion.   An excellent use of primary sources which, for most researchers, would be lost in a mass of available documents. 263-277.

267 Bernstein, Barton J.   "Syngman Rhee: The Pawn as Rook: The Struggle to End the Korean War" Bulletin of Concerned Asian Scholars 10 (January-March 1978) 38-45.
Traces the history of President Rhee's efforts to block a peace agreement and force a military solution to the unification question.   Ridgway's concern is discussed as well as his objections to Washington over Rhee's behavior.

268 Bohlen, Celestine. "Advice to Stalin: Hold Korean War P. O. W.'s" The New York Times International Page (September 25, 1952) 142:A6
In a long article the author reports that Stalin's advice to the Chinese and Korean Communist leaders was to keep twenty per cent of the captured American pilots to be used as bargaining tokens in future diplomatic negotiations.

269 "Climax in Korea" US News 32 (May 9, 1952) 15-17.
The war in Korea has reached that significant point where the UN can either accept a truce, or they can move on to more intense fighting. Ridgway says the war can go either way, depending on the Chinese.

270   "Continued Stalemate on Korean Cease-Fire" United Nations Bulletin 11:6 (September 15, 1951) 276-277.
Ridgway, angered over stalled talks, tells the Chinese he is still interested and willing to negotiate.

271   "The Course of Negotiations for a Cease-Fire in Korea" United Nations Bulletin 11:4 (August 15, 1951) 149.
The cease-fire negotiations were suspended again over the violation of the neutralized zone. Ridgway, in a broadcast 4 August, 1951, suggests the talks begin again.

272   "Diplomacy by Publicity" Newsweek 38 (July 1951) 26.
This short but very informative article discusses the public nature of the Ridgway armistice proposal. The article provides a chronology of the peace efforts and Ridgway's role of "publicity" in pushing toward some sort of negotiated truce in Korea.

273   "Diplomatic Front" Time 58 (July 9, 1951) 21.
Suggests the Red's are now willing to talk peace and announces Ridgway will offer them an invitation.

274   "Efforts to Agree on Conditions for Resuming Cease-Fire Talks" United Nations Bulletin 11:7 (October 1, 1951).
Ridgway makes a new proposal in an effort to end stalemate; willing to close discussion over previous disagreements and begin a new set of talks.

275   "General in a Hurry" Newsweek 33 (July 16, 1951) 311.
Discusses Ridgway's opening of peace negotiations in Korea while carrying on his duties in Japan.

276   "Korean Truce Talks Resume at Pan Mun Jon" United Nations Bulletin 11:9 (November 1, 1951).
Ridgway admits that there were two United Nations air violations of the neutral zone. He offered an official apology, citing the difficulty of being sure all units were informed of the move.

277   "New Proposals in Prisoners in Korean Cease-Fire Talks" United Nations Bulletin 12:2 (January 15, 1952) 72-73.
     As the early discussion of prisoner exchange is underway, Ridgway makes a "personal request" to North Korean Premier Kim Il Sung, that the Red Cross be allowed to make on site inspections of prisoner of war camps.

278 "New Site Chosen for Korean Cease-Fire Talk" United Nations Bulletin 11:8 (October 15, 1951) 339-340, 344.
     As a result of Ridgway's suggestion the location of the talks was moved to "Pan Mun Jon" where both sides can provide better security for the conference neutrality.

279   "New United Nations Commander in Korea Visits Headquarters" United Nations Bulletin 12:9 (May 1, 1952) 421.
     Secretary-General Trygve Lie makes comments on Ridgway's role as a "magnificent contribution to the United Nations program of collective security in Korea."

280 "No Progress Reported in Korean Cease-fire Talks" United Nations Bulletin 12:3 (February 1, 1952) 113.
     Ridgway accuses the North Koreans of not providing adequate air raid protection for United Nations prisoners in camps.

281   "North Korean Chinese Communist's Charges Bring Second Halt in Cease-Fire Talks" United Nations Bulletin 11:5 (September 1, 1951) 218-219.
     A message, 23 August, to Ridgway from Kim Il Sung claims that the United Nations had broken the neutrality of the conference zone. Ridgway suggests that an investigation has been conducted and there is no truth to the charge.

282 "Progress of the Negotiations for Cease-Fire in Korea" United Nations Bulletin 11:10 (November 15, 1951) 408-409.
     Ridgway makes yet another proposal on a new armistice line for ending the Korean War.

283   "Progress of the Talks for a Korean Cease-Fire"
United Nations Bulletin 11:12 (December 1, 1951) 512-
515.
  As talks continue, the questions Ridgway's group
must face now concern the size of remaining armies, and
some sort of on-site inspection.

284   "Story of Negotiations for a Korean Cease-Fire"
United Nations Bulletin 11:3 (August 1, 1951) 94-95+.
  One aspect of Ridgway's efforts to set up cease-
fire discussion, concerned allowing newspersons to the
neutralized conference area.

285   "Washington Again Talks, Moves To Speed Red Accord
on Truce" Newsweek 39 (April 14, 1952) 46.
  "Ridgway -- Commander of Plague Parasites" responds
to charges amidst push for truce talks.

286   "Wish for Peaceful Settlement Constantly Stressed
in Korea: General Ridgway's Final Report" United Nations
Bulletin 10:4 (June 1, 1951) 511-512.
  Ridgway reports the Chinese Communist Forces are on
the defensive and confirms atrocities still continue.

NATO Commander

BOOKS

287   Jordan, Robert S. (editor).   Generals in
International Politics: NATO's Supreme Allied
Commanders, Europe.   Louisville, Kentucky: The
University Press of Kentucky, 1987. 229 pages, index,
photographs.
  An excellent study of the political role of those
generals who have held, or served in, the NATO Command.
Very significant look at Ridgway who played an important
part in bringing NATO into reality.   Because of
Ridgway's significant role he can be found throughout
the book.   However, chapter two "Trying to Make Good on
the Promises" is most helpful.

288   NATO -- Its Development and Significance.
Washington, DC: United States Department of State
Publication Number 4630, General Foreign Policy Series,
1952.
    A brief discussion of the problems faced by NATO as
it began to function in Europe after the war, it
includes an analysis of General Ridgway's role in the
organization of a reliable military division which,
prior to that time, had existed only on paper.
Especially see page 20.

ARTICLES

289   "Change in Command: NATO" Time 59 (May 5, 1952)
30.
    In a brief but informative announcement General
Ridgway's new appointment is identified, along with
comment on the difficulty in succeeding Eisenhower at
SHAPE.

290   "General Ridgway Assumes SHAPE Command" Department
of State Bulletin (May 12, 1952) 743.
    Statement by the President Truman, and released by
the White House, 28 April, 1952, in which he announces
the appointment of Matthew B. Ridgway to replace
Eisenhower as Supreme Allied Commander.

291   "The Generals Sound Off" New Republic (October
13, 1952) 6.
    Ridgway was furious at the amount of red tape
created by the French. He blows up at Defense Minister
Rene Pleven who he feels creates unnecessary
difficulties. In the meantime Marshal Juin, Commander
of NATO ground forces in Central Europe, turns his anger
on the Americans, suggesting that at times they act like
Russia. Shows another side of Ridgway and to the
problems he faces in his new command.

292   Hauser, Earnest O.   "Ridgway's Toughest Job"
Saturday Evening Post (October 25, 1952) 22-23, 84-92.
    Really is posed as a question. Can Ridgway, fresh
from the shooting war in Korea, plagued by the
diplomatic subtleties of a European command, and lacking
Eisenhower's enormous prestige, run the show for NATO?
In a long and well written account, Hauser responds that
it will be different than Ike, but probably as well
done. Ridgway's job is to counter the old pre-Korea
apathy that gripped the United States. Excellent in
terms of information and analysis.

293 Kaplan, Lawrence S. "The Korean War and the U. S.
Foreign Relations: The Case of NATO" Heller, Francis H.
(editor).   The Korean War: A Twenty Five Year
Perspective. Lawrence, Kansas: The Regents Press of
Kansas, 1977. 251 pages, index, photographs.
    Truman saw the invasion of Korea as the beginning
of World War III and felt that only a constant response
to any challenge would prevent total war. And, because
of both his leadership and his pressure on the United
Nations, America emerged as a military world power. An
emergence, Kaplan seems to assume, resulted more from
the Korean War than World War II. The fact that the
armistice held, and containment worked in this limited
case, supports his theory. Interesting analysis of a
period in which Ridgway was very active in American and
NATO affairs. 36-75.

294   LaFeber, Walter. "NATO and the Korean War: A
Context" Diplomatic History 13:4 (Fall 1989) 461-477.
    Discusses the Korean War in light of the United
States obligations to NATO, assuming that the war in
Korea is a war with the "second team", the primary enemy
remains the Soviet Union.

295 "Man in Mid-Passage" Time 59 (June 2, 1952) 16.
    Announces General Ridgway's appointment to SHAPE.
Discusses Ridgway's concern over the communist build-up
during the peace talks in Korea.

296   "Man on His Way Over . . . Man on His Way Back"
Life   32 (June 2, 1952) 23-27.
      Ridgway makes his way to West Point to receive his
second oak-leaf cluster to his Distinguished Service
Medal, and then back to Paris to become an honorary
citizen of Louveciennes near SHAPE headquarters.

297   Millis, Walter. "General Gruenther's Headaches"
Colliers   (July 11, 1953) 9-11.
      This interesting article reports to deal with
Gruenther, but is a brief and excellent comment on
Ridgway's time as commander of NATO forces.   Is in
strong support of Ridgway's contribution.

298   "New NATO, U. N. Chiefs"   Senior Scholastic   60
(May 7, 1952) 13.
      Announces that Ridgway, appointed by President
Truman, was named at the request of the North Atlantic
Council.

299   "New Pentagon Team"   New York Times Sunday Magazine
(July 24, 1953) 6-7.
      Addresses the new defense team, with considerable
emphasis on the variety of personalities (including
Ridgway) represented in this balance between civilian
control and military accountability.

300   "People of the Week"   US News   30 (April 20, 1951)
41.
      Ridgway leaves policy in Korea to the Joint Chiefs
as he heads for a new assignment as Supreme Commander of
the Allied Powers.

301   "Ridgway Replaces Eisenhower In NATO's Supreme
Command"   Newsweek   39 (May 5, 1952) 36.
      Lists General Ridgway's credentials for the job,
then suggests both the "why of Ridgway" centering on his
acceptance by military and political leaders alike; and
the "how of Ridgway" which is summarized by a quote from
the Japanese: "Ridgway's administration has been so
evenly conducted and he is so unobtrusive it is
difficult to think of him except officially.

302   "Ridgway -- Target of Communists"   US News 34 (March 27, 1953) 18-19.
Ridgway is the target of a whispering campaign which is assumed to have been masterminded by the communists to undermine his effectiveness at NATO.

303 "Weakness Beclouds Strength In a U.S. Presidential Year" Newsweek 39 (May 26, 1952) 25.
Ridgway's move to NATO occurs just as another crisis between Moscow and Washington is developing.

304   Winner, Percy. "Ridgway Takes Command"   New Republic (May 19, 1952) 9.
Ridgway took command at NATO with some serious opposition, but that is changing. Basically a support for Ridgway, who in assuming his new role, will clash with the Russians.

Chief of Staff

BOOKS

305   Bell, William Gardner.   Commanding Generals and Chiefs of Staff: Portraits and Biographical Sketches. Washington, DC: Chief of Military History, 1992.
This second edition includes the reproduction of an oil painting of General Ridgway, plus a short but inclusive biography of his military service. 128-129.

306   Condit, Doris M. History of the Office of the Secretary of Defense, Vol II, The Test of War, 1950-1953. Washington, DC: History Office, Office of the Secretary of Defense, 1988. Index.
The relationship between the Secretary of Defense and the Joint Chief is considered as well as Ridgway's role at NATO, the industrial-military complex, European versus Asian priorities, and other Ridgway related items all indexed.

307   Poole, Walter.   History of the Joint Chiefs of Staff: The Joint Chiefs of Staff and National Policy, 1950-1952. Volume 4. Washington, DC: History Division, Joint Chiefs of Staff, 1979. Index.

This official version of the Joint Chiefs has a good deal of information about Ridgway both as a general responding to their direction, and as the army chief of staff. See index.

308   Schnabel, James F. and Robert G. Watson. History of the Joint Chiefs of Staff: The Joint Chiefs of Staff and National Policy. Volume 3. Washington, DC: History Division, Part 1 - 1978, Part 2 - 1979.

Contains a lot of information dealing with the planning, and execution of war policy during the Korean War, thus is essential to Ridgway scholars. Produced in soft cover and duplicated by the Historical Division, Joint Secretariat, Joint Chiefs of Staff, it is available through Modern Military History Headquarters, National Archives.

309   Soldiers and Statesmen: Proceedings of the Fourth Military Symposium, U. S. A. F. Academy, Colorado Springs, 1970.

The account of this symposium looks at the various roles played by military leaders whose responsibilities placed them within the political arena. General Ridgway clearly expresses his view that there is an imbalance in the Armed Forces, with far too much dependence on air power and technology, and far too little understanding of the necessity of ground troops. 157-159.

310   Watson, Robert G.   History of the Joint Chiefs of Staff: The Joint Chiefs and National Policy, 1953-1954. Volume 5. Washington, DC: History Division, Joint Chiefs of Staff, 1986. Index.

Ridgway's role as a member of the Joint Chiefs is evident in this brief but valuable history. It acknowledges his belief in a flexible national policy (40); his role in Korea (230-244); in the negotiations (56); view on Vietnam (253); and dozens of other topics all indexed.

ARTICLES

311   Abel, Elie.   "The Joint Chiefs"   New York Times Sunday Magazine   (Feb 6, 1953) 9-11.
Differences come out between members of the Joint Chiefs, particularly over the intervention of China if there was an attack on Formosa. The absolute role of the President (the civilian source) in such matters was affirmed.

312   "Chief of Staff"   Army Information Digest   8:8 (August 1953) 35.
Picture and brief biographical description of the new members of the Joint Chiefs of Staff.

313   "It's the Old Postwar Story -- Army Cut Again" US News   36 (February 12, 1954) 48+.
Yielding to orders, but with many misgivings, General Ridgway is making a deep cut in the size of the armed forces. America still need ground troops.

314   "The Long Haul"   Time   66 (July 25, 1955) 11.
Despite General Ridgway's letter to the Chief of Staff, army forces will be cut by Congress.

315   "A Matter of Perspective" Time   65 (February 14, 1955) 18.
Ridgway testifies that the current defense bill will hurt the army and endanger American security.

316   "The New Brass"   Time   61 (May 25, 1953) 21.
Introduces the new Chiefs of Staff, Admiral Radford, Admiral Carney, General Gruenther and General Ridgway. Short biographical sketches of each.

317   "The New Chief of Staff"   Army Combat Forces Journal   4 (September 1953) 8-9.
A brief account of Matthew B. Ridgway as Commander of the US Eighth Army in Korea, and his European Command.

318   "The New Military Team" Newsweek 41 (May 25, 1953) 31.
       Introduces General Ridgway, Admiral Carney, General Twining, and General Gruenther as the new Chiefs of Staff.

319   "People of the Week" US News 34 (May 22, 1953) 50.
       The new Joint Chiefs are the personal choice of the President and are the key to revised strategy.

320   "People of the Week" US News 35 (December 18, 1953) 14.
       As the new Chief of Staff, Ridgway finds himself being ordered to cut the armed forces.

321   "People of the Week" US News 36 (March 26, 1954) 16.
       Ridgway tells Congress of his concern over current defense postures, and reflects a concern over the lack of unity in the Joint Chiefs.

322   "Ridgway and the New Warfare" The Commonweal 61 (February 18, 1955) 314.
       Supports Ridgway's argument for retaining a serious conventional army, and not relying on technical weapons too heavily.

323   "Ridgway's Misgivings" America 93 (July 30, 1955) 426.
       While Ridgway writes "the military advisor role of a member of the Joint Chiefs of Staff was limited to giving professional military advice" he joins in the battle between defense cuts and a strong army. Ridgway suggests the president's views are "parochial".

324   "The Sidelong Look" Time 63 (March 29, 1954) 16.
       When testifying before Congress Ridgway gave the "proper" answer when asked about army cuts. But indicated he felt a strong army was needed.

325   "What Gen. Ridgway Finds Wrong with U. S. Defenses"
US News   39 (July 29, 1955) 70-74.
     Text of General Ridgway's letter to Secretary of
Defense Charles Wilson, in which he suggests that
nuclear weapons are not sufficient to win wars, and
supports a strong army.

326   "Why US Steers Clear of a Fight in Asia"   US News
37 (December 19, 1954) 62+.
     General Ridgway, holding that the foot soldier
still is war's decisive factor, argues that his army is
not strong enough to support intervention in Asia.
Eisenhower supports him at this time.

Tactics, Lessons

BOOKS

327   Asprey, Robert.   War of Shadows: The History of
Guerilla Warfare.   New York: MacMillan, 1952.
     Wonders if the Joint Chiefs and the President's
advisors were ignorant of Ridgway's 1954 report, or
simply ignored it.   A proper understanding of this
caution may well have saved America from "the worst
miscalculation in our history".

328   Bolger, Daniel P.   Leavenworth Papers, Number 19,
Scenes from an Unfinished War: Low-Intensity Conflict in
Korea, 1966-1969.   Fort Leavenworth, Kansas: Combat
Studies Institute, Government Printing Office, 1991. 163
pages, index, photographs, maps, bibliography.
     A careful study of the military and political
situation left over from the first of America's
"unfinished wars".   Excellent discussion of the
situation as it was left in Korea, and what the United
States has done about it.   Includes a listing of armed
encounters during the period of the study.   An
interesting report when taken with Ridgway's general
predictions.

329 Foot, Rosemary. The Wrong War: American Policy and Dimension of The Korean Conflict, 1950-1953. Ithaca, New York: Cornell University Press, 1958. 290 pages, index.
This very significant discussion of American involvement in Korea discusses Ridgway's part in planning for the experience of the war, his involvement in war leadership, and his requests for permission to bomb Manchuria. 146-149, 154-155, 177, 240f.

330 Gavin, James M. War and Peace in the Space Age. New York: Harper & Brothers, Publishers, 1958. 304 pages, index, map.
Writing after the close of his military career, Gavin provides a "past as prologue" look at America at war and peace. He references Ridgway on numerous occasions, primarily dealing with the question of military preparedness. Not a lot new but gives us Gavin's perspective, references indexed.

331 Kaufman, Burton I. The Korean War: Challenges in Crisis, Credibility, and Command. Philadelphia: Temple University Press, 1986. 381 pages, index, maps.
This study of the political and military implications of the Korean War suggest that not only did the US not understand what was going on during the war, but drew all the wrong conclusions from what happened there. He assumes the revisionist school and the belief that the Korean War, more than World War II, marked US reentry into the world wide military struggle. There is heavy reference to Ridgway, but he is well indexed.

332 Marshall, Samuel L. A., Cate Marshall (editor). Bringing Up the Rear: A Memoir. San Francisco: Presidio Press, 1979. 310 pages, index, photographs, maps.
Marshall, one of the most respected military historians, saw military service for over thirty years and wrote its history. This account discusses his meetings with, and great respect for Ridgway in both Europe and Korea. Of primary significance is his discussion of Ridgway's use of the military analyzer - the historian as tactician. 93-94, 187-209.

333   O'Ballance, Edgar.   Korea: 1950-1953. Hamden,
Connecticut: Archon Books. 171 pages, index, maps.
    Sees Ridgway as highly critical of intelligence
operations. Especially chapter six, "Ridgway's Counter
Offensive".

ARTICLES

334   Bradley, Omar N.   "US Military Policy: 1950"
Reader's Digest (October 1950).
    The Chairman of the Joint Chief of Staff
acknowledges the shift taking place in American policy
in Korea, that is, from containment to contesting
communism.

335 Braestrup, Peter. "The Korean War" Battle Lines:
Report of the Twentieth Fund Task Force on the Military
and the Media. New York: Priority Press Publishers,
1985. 47-60.
    Discusses censorship during the Korean War,
including Ridgway's use of media control, his directions
about and response to the media, as well as his general
attitude concerning censorship and the media.

336   Cottrell, Alvin J. and James E. Dougherty. "The
Lessons of Korea: War and the Power of Man" Orbis
(April-May 1958) for Policy Research Institute. 39-64.
    An interesting account of the impact of limited war,
and the failure of the United States to see the Korean
conflict in light of the strategic background.
Discusses Ridgway's concern over the establishment of a
cease-fire line too early in the negotiations.

337   "Cry Peace" The Commonweal 62 (July 29, 1955)
414.
    Identifies the fact that Ridgway and the
administration defense policies have been at sharp odds.
The editorial supports Ridgway, and the need for a
strong defense budget. "Wilson may be able to shrug off
General Ridgway's criticism of Administration policy; we
cannot."

338 "I Have Been Shot at From Ambush..." New Republic 134 (January 23, 1956) 3.
     The title identifies Ridgway's comment when President Eisenhower released his 1954 State of the Union message. Eisenhower suggested he had received a unanimous recommendation by the Joint Chiefs of Staff. Ridgway had taken serious exception to the defense budget, which he discussed with Eisenhower and felt he had been betrayed.

339 Ruetten, Richard T. "General Douglas MacArthur's 'Reconnaissance in Force': The Rationalization of a Defeat in Korea" Pacific Historical Review   36 (February 1967) 79-89.
     In this well documented analysis the author, a San Diego historian, suggests that the division of Eighth Army and X Corps was a major mistake, and that the failure to coordinate X Corps and Eighth Army responses along the Yalu -- a mistake MacArthur hid as a "reconnaissance in force" -- was a major defeat for the United Nations and for MacArthur.

340 West, Philip. "Interpreting the Korean War" The American Historical Review 94 (February 1989) 80-96.
     This is a combined review of six major Korean War books which Philip West identified as representing the changing nature of historical efforts which, -- taking a phrase from Arthur Schlesinger, Jr., -- have moved from the "heroic stage to the academic stage". He views the revisionist writings of the war premature as the real sources of information, North Korean and Chinese sources are still very limited.

341 Witze, C. "Defense Cuts USAF Budget $1-2 Billion" Aviation Week 64 (January 30, 1956) 32.
     Discusses Ridgway's concern about the reduction of military funds especially in light of the threat of limited war contingencies. Reflects Ridgway's willingness to be put into direct conflict with the civilian authorities of the Armed Forces.

Following Retirement

BOOKS

342 Brown, Weldon A. Prelude to Disaster: The American Role in Vietnam, 1940-1963. Port Washington, New York: Kennikat Press, 1975. 278 pages, index.
    Reflects on General Ridgway's view on American unpreparedness for the Vietnam War and on the affirmation that diplomacy in Asia would have to be supported by military presence. America was ill prepared for such an intense and prolonged war. 53-54, 95.

343   MacDonald, Callum A.   Korea: The War Before Vietnam. New York: The Free Press, 1986. 330 pages, index, photographs, bibliography.
    The author views Korea as the initial phase of the Vietnam experience. He considered the US policy of a limited war to be a failure and one re-played in Vietnam. Ridgway's view of limited war is considered, indexed.

344 The Pentagon Papers. The Senator Gavel Edition, Boston: Beacon Press, in 4 volumes of documents, 1 volume of essay, 1971-1972. Index.
    Primary documents of the Vietnam War released against State Department wishes during the anti-Vietnam debates. Documents Ridgway's role in opposing American involvement in Vietnam (I:55) his advice to President Johnson concerning withdrawal (IV:591), and a report on Ridgway's visit to Indochina (I:127, I:92 and IV:267).

345 Wexler, Sanford. The Vietnam War: An Eyewitness History. New York: Facts on File, 1992.
    This is a well done view of the Vietnam War from inception to retreat. The Ridgway reference is short and available from other sources but it puts the Korean Commander's antagonism to the war in its proper perspective. 44.

ARTICLES

346 "Brass in Business: Gen. Ridgway Next?" Newsweek 45 (May 2, 1955) 65-66.
   In considering General Ridgway's retirement the article looks at high ranking soldiers who have retired into major business positions.

347 "Nuclear Wars Can Be Small" Life 39 (July 25, 1955) 26.
   Ridgway, on retiring, points out that massive retaliation is not the only kind of war contemplated by the US. Ground forces are still necessary.

348 "People of the Week" US News 40 (January 27, 1956) 14.
   Ridgway, now retired and chairman of an industrial group, still feels it is unwise to make a public statement about his view of army appropriations.

349 "Ridgway's Biggest Battle ... for Troops, Not Machines" Newsweek 44 (July 26, 1954) 20.
   Ridgway urges the President not to interfere in Vietnam; while pushing for more ground troops for the "small wars".

350 "What Ridgway Told Ike" US News 36 (June 25, 1954) 30-32.
   Speaking about America avoiding involvement in the Vietnam War, he tells the President that air power cannot win it, and it will be a ground war which would make the Korean War seem simple by comparison.

351 "Women Warriors: A Shift to Barbarism?" Army Times (February 26, 1979) 17.
   General Ridgway's voice joins the argument over the role of women in the military. He makes few points when he affirms "the growing reliance on women threatens the spirit and effectiveness of our armed forces . . . ".

OTHER SOURCES

Dissertations and Information Papers

352   Busch, Terry J.   "A Comparative Cross-Service
'Operational Code' Analysis of the 'Military Mind'
Concept: The Post World War II American Military
Profession" Ph.D. dissertation, Miami University, 1975,
317 pages. See Chapter Three.
    An attempt to identify formulas of military
thinking based on a study of career development and
crisis decision making.

353 Flint, Roy Kenneth. "The Tragic Flaw: MacArthur,
The Joint Chiefs, and the Korean War" Ph.D.
dissertation, Duke University, 1976.
    Only peripherally concerned with Ridgway, but
significant in that it includes a powerful study of the
failure of command, and the persistence on outmoded
concepts of command relationships between higher
headquarters, theater, and field commanders. Very
critical of MacArthur.

354 Hackett, John L. "The General and the President:
A Conflict in Strategies" Student Paper, US Army War
College, USAWC Library. March 1989, 51 pages.
    This study is primarily concerned with MacArthur's
role, and his difference with President Truman. However
Hackett deals with Ridgway as a part of his study of
command conflict.

355 Hakon, Ostholm. "The First Year of the Korean War:
The Road Toward Armistice" Ph.D. dissertation, Kent
State University, 1982. 267 pages.
    Holds that the Korean War was the most catastrophic
of the international conflicts. The event created a
situation no one wanted. Chapter four deals with the
effect of this view on the fighting of the war, and
discusses the dangers seen by the military leadership
involved in the war.

356   Hermes, Walter G. "The United States Army in the Korean War: The Last Two Years, July 1951-July 1953", Ph.D. dissertation, Georgetown University, 1966.
This very interesting work takes a look at the fact the US Army was given executive responsibility for carrying out military policy in Korea, and for negotiating the truce agreement. The armistice, originally designed as a military tool, became a political document drawn up with military leaders; Ridgway especially, assuming political and diplomatic matters.

357   Lofgren, Stephen.   "LTG Matthew Ridgway's Information Policy during the Korean War"   Chief Military History Information Paper, 7 November 1990. Bibliography Files.   Training Command, Information. Command and General Staff College, Ft. Leavenworth, Kansas.

358   Lofgren, Stephen.   "Nonconcurrence by U. S. Army Chiefs of Staff with National Military Strategy: General Matthew B. Ridgway and General Maxwell Taylor"   Chief Military History Information Paper, 5 December 1990. Miscellaneous Files. Command and General Staff College, Ft. Leavenworth, Kansas.
Interesting study which, following the title premise, takes a serious look at disagreements between the leading military spokespersons and the national strategy as represented by the president.

359 Ohn, Chang-Il. "The Joint Chiefs of Staff and U. S. Policy and Strategy Regarding Korea, 1945-1953" Ph.D. dissertation, University of Kansas, 1983. 465 pages.
In a policy running from indifference to reluctance, the Joint Chiefs internationalized the war, and sought the armistice as a means by which they could "scuttle and run" from Korea. Up to and including the Eisenhower administration, the Joint Chiefs (including Ridgway) operated on a policy of "no-win" in which they could remain in Korea without winning the war.

360 Pelletier, Eugene. "The Ridgway Regime at SHAPE: A Preliminary History" Masters Thesis, Georgetown University, March 1955.
    An early, but significant look, at the role Ridgway played as commander, and at the political aspects of Ridgway's career. Especially interesting is chapter two.

361 Weiss, Lawrence Stephen. "Story Around the Cradle: The Korean War and the Early Years of the People's Republic of China, 1949-1953" Ph.D. dissertation, Columbia University. Michigan: University Microfilm International.
    Discusses Ridgway's method of challenging the Chinese People's Army (92-93) and his determination to kill rather than to occupy (226-228).

Films

362 Aircombat Video Collection. Clifton, New Jersey: US News Video, 1989-1991, 13 cassettes, 50 minutes, sound, color and black and white, 1/2 inch. V1 Airborne, V7 Parachute, V8 Paratroopers, V12 World War II, Europe.

363 Air Drop at Arnhem. The War Years, Part 18, 30 minutes, black and white, 16 mm. D-16.
    Pictured is the disastrous British-American parachute attempt during World War II.

364 Korea: The Forgotten War. Library Video Company, sound, black and white. Distributed Library Video.

365 Korea: MacArthur's War. MP1518, 60 minutes, sound, black and white. Distributed MPI Home Video.

366 A Motion Picture History of the Korean War. Washington, DC: Department of Defense, 1981, 58 minutes, sound, black and white. Distributed by National Audio-Visual Center.

367   United States Army, 82nd Airborne.   <u>Airborne at
War</u>.   Nashville,   Tennessee: Cumberland   Marketing
International, 199? [sic] Video, 76 minutes, black and
white, 1/2 inch.

INDEX OF
PERIODICALS REVIEWED

Naval War College Review
Negro History Bulletin
New American Mercury
New Republic
New Statesman and Nation
New York Times Book Review
New York Times Magazine
Newsweek
Orbis
Pacific Affairs
Pacific Historical Review
Pacific Spectator
Parents
Pegasus
Pointer
Political Affairs
Political Quarterly
Political Science Quarterly
Presidential Studies Quarterly
Prologue
Public Administration Review
Public Interest
Public Opinion Quarterly
Quartermaster Review
Reader's Digest
Reporter
Reviews in American History
Review of Politics
Rocky Mountain Social Science Journal

Saturday Evening Post
Senior Scholastic
Signal
Social Problems
Studies in History and Society
Studies on the Soviet Union
Time
Twentieth Century
United Nations Bulletin
United National World
United Services and Empire Review
United States Armed Forces Medical Journal
United States Naval Institute Proceedings
US Air Service
US Army Aviation Digest
US News and World Report
Utah History Quarterly
Ventures
Virginia Quarterly Review
Vital Speeches
Western Pennsylvania History Magazine
Wilson Quarterly
Wisconsin Magazine of History
World Affairs

AUTHOR INDEX

Unless noted, numbers refer to entries.

SUBJECT INDEX

Unless noted, number refer to entries.

About the Compiler

PAUL M. EDWARDS, Dean of the Graduate College of Park College in Kansas City, Missouri, is a specialist in Korean, military, and bibliographical history who has written at length on these subjects. He is the founder of the Center for Study of the Korean Conflict, a library and archival foundation in Independence, Missouri. He served with the 31st Field Artillery in Korea and has his Ph.D. in transatlantic history from the University of St. Andrews in Scotland.